CRIMES OF NARRATION

CAMUS' *LA CHUTE*

Alex Argyros

For Uri Eisenzweig who
convinced me to put my
thoughts on paper, and Amy
Argyros without whom I could
not have done it.

© 1985 Alex Argyros, Éditions Paratexte, Trinity College,
Toronto, Canada M5S 1H8

ISBN 0-920615-04-X

INTRODUCTION

THE day is long past when the literary critic could view his craft as unproblematic. In the past several decades, a large and complex body of critical thought, much of it originating in France, has, if it has accomplished nothing else, made it impossible to ignore the question of critical point of view. The nonchalance borne of confidence in one's neutrality, that is, the comfortable invisibility a critic assumes when he pretends to allow the text to speak in its own voice, has been troubled by the growing awareness that the critic's perspective will, to a large extent, determine what he sees.

I do not believe that critical methodology is the sole creator of meaning in a literary text. That argument, that literature is an infinitely malleable field whose pure effervescent textuality precludes no interpretation, is, I think, a vestige of that romantic attachment to an original state of pure, unstructured potential which philosophers such as Jacques Derrida have been trying to question. Neither, however, do I think that a literary text contains a message hidden inside it, like a baby in a mother's womb. The critic is neither father nor midwife.

If the critic is neither the author of the text he analyzes nor the vehicle whereby some pre-formed meaning gets expressed, what is his function? My reading of *La Chute* will be guided by the following presuppositions:

A. The text will be treated like an artifact. I will not concern myself with Camus' intentions. I do not know what Camus' real intentions were and ultimately, although I may be personally curious about the historical figure indicated by the words *Albert Camus*, his intentions would have no bearing on my interpretation of his novel[1]. Having written *La Chute*,

---

1. I emphasize the word *real*. We have of course, many accounts by

Camus became one reader among others.

B. *La Chute's* fictionality will be respected. Jean-Baptiste Clamence is not a real person, so to discuss his psychological states, for example, would be to violate the specific nature of *La Chute* – that it is a work of fiction[2].

C. Meaning will not be deployed according to level. It is fairly commonplace in criticism inspired by an amalgamation of Structuralism and Freudian Psychoanalysis to look for a manifest structure which the critic undermines by demonstrating that it is constituted by a more fundamental, though less accessible, bed of subjacent structures. Perhaps the clearest formulation of this critical strategy in Camusian studies is Costes', for whom the literary text is like a patient insofar as both are a mixture of consciousness and unconsciousness. In the first chapter of *Albert Camus ou la parole manquante*, he establishes certain guidelines:

Camus of his novels. For example, in his « Prière d'insérer » to *La Chute* he says : « *L'homme qui parle dans* La Chute *se livre à une confession calculée. Réfugié à Amsterdam dans une ville de canaux et de lumière froide, où il joue à l'ermite et au prophète, cet ancien avocat attend dans un bar douteux des auditeurs complaisants. § Il a le cœur moderne, c'est-à-dire qu'il ne peut supporter d'être jugé. Il se dépêche donc de faire son propre procès mais c'est pour mieux juger les autres. Le miroir dans lequel il se regarde, il finit par le tendre aux autres. § Où commence la confession, où l'accusation? Celui qui parle dans ce lieu fait-il son procès, ou celui de son temps? Est-il un cas particulier, ou l'homme du jour? Une seule vérité en tout cas, dans ce jeu de glaces étudié : la douleur, et ce qu'elle promet.* » (in *Théâtre, récits, nouvelles*, [Paris, Gallimard, « Bibliothèque de la Pléiade », 1962], p. 2006).

2. Others do not share this critical prejudice. Many readers of *La Chute* persist in discussing Clamence as if he were a human being. Some, like Brian Masters, speculate about Clamence's motivations (for example, "*We must become a little better acquainted with Clamence before deciding what were Camus' intentions in creating such a destructive man.*" [*Camus : A Study* (Totowa, New Jersey, Rowman and Littlefield, 1974), p. 119]) in order to divine Camus' intentions ; others, such as Alain Costes (*Albert Camus ou la parole manquante. Étude psychanalytique* [Paris, Payot, 1973]) are more inclined towards a psychoanalytic approach towards Camus' protagonist.

À s'en tenir à notre préambule, l'analyse d'une œuvre écrite pourrait ne pas différer beaucoup de celle d'un patient : puisque l'inconscient est un invariant, l'ensemble conceptuel dégagé à partir de la relation analysé-analyste peut être transposé en bloc à cette « relation » où l'analysé est soit une œuvre, soit son auteur, soit encore les deux.[3]

Since I refuse to ponder Camus' original intentions (conscious or unconscious), all I am left with is *La Chute*. Like any literary text, it produces meaning in a variety of ways. Meaning results from the word it disposes, from the events it describes, from the characters it creates, from the description of these events and characters and simply from its status as "literature" in our culture. I will not, of course, describe every way in which *La Chute* creates meaning. Such a goal requires an omniscient critic who is not that different from the neutral critic who assumes he can simply allow the text to express itself. My focus is limited and idiosyncratic. It is constituted in part by those thinkers who have most influenced me : Freud, Heidegger and Derrida (Freud by his attention to detail, Heidegger by his dissection of the history and historicity of the concept of truth and Derrida by his speculations on writing). Therefore, although I am in principle unable to describe all the ways in which *La Chute* creates meaning, I will not compensate for my limits by privileging certain layers of meaning which are possibly of my own creation. In fact, I maintain that literature has no levels. It is not an analysand, nor is it a palimpsest. Literature is flat, it is all surface. A literary text may seek to privilege certain of the meanings it produces and it is undeniable that the words and narrative structures of a novel favour the production of certain meanings at the expense of others. To argue otherwise, as I have previously suggested, would be to make of the literary text a purely passive receptacle for the critic's sallies. Every literary text produces meaning hierarchically. Such hierarchies will be respected. But heirarchy does not

3. *Op. cit.*, p. 15.

mean level. All the elements constitutive of a hierarchy are clearly visible. Levels, on the other hand, imply the metaphysics of interiority. Unless the notion of level is taken as purely geometric, to speak of levels of meaning is usually to employ such metaphors as interior-exterior, latent-manifest, content-container etc., all of which, I maintain, violate the strange and often bewildering simplicity of literature.

D. Criticism is reading. Like all reading, criticism is the production of meaning. There is no meaning in an unread text. However, that is not to say that meaning is produced freely by the reader. Reading literature is analogous to experiencing the world. I take as my model for reading the phenomenology of Edmund Husserl. Although the following is a gross simplification of a highly complex structure, it could be argued that Husserl divides the act of perception into three parts : noesis, noema and hyle[4]. Noesis is intentionality. It is the subject's thrust into the world. Noema is the world as represented to the subject. Hyle is that part of the world which does not depend on the subject, that brute materiality which limits the subject's interpretations. Similarly, reading is divided into three components. The reader imports into the text a battery of personal and cultural biases. The text itself is meaningful within a certain historical context. And the text has a hyletic component, a core of meaning which is resistant to cultural and historical transformations. My reading of *La Chute*, therefore, will be, in essence, tripartite. What I see in the text will be an amalgamation of structures which are a-historical, those which are subject to the whims of culture and those which derive their significance from the historical consciousness which I am.

---

4. The best translation of *Ideen Zu Einer Reiner Phänomenologie Und Phänomenoligischen Philosophie* is Paul Ricœur's, *Idées directrices pour une phénoménologie* (Paris, Gallimard, 1950). See especially Chapter III, « Noèse et Noème », pp. 300-35.

MEXICO-CITY

LA CHUTE is a monologue. Specifically it is a seduction. The narrator, initially simply "I", accosts an unnamed interlocutor in a seedy bar in Amsterdam. The novel to follow is a confession in six parts, a confession whose first person narration is interrupted only by holes in the text the responses to which form a strange, one-sided dialogue. Like many characters in Camus' novels, the interlocutor in *La Chute* is characterized by silence[1].

Although, as we shall see, the interlocutor's taciturnity clearly allows Clamence the latitude to make his condemnation of the human race general, initially I would like to stress the simple fact of his silence.

The interlocutor is not the only silent character in the novel. In fact, if what inaugurates the novel is a seduction, the means for that seduction is another silent figure. Specifically, the narrator offers his services to his unnamed quarry because the bartender of *Mexico-City* speaks only Dutch and precious little of that. The bartender, alternately called Ape, Cro-Magnon Man and Cave Man, is characterized by his inarticulateness. Half man, half beast, his inability to manipulate language is in sharp contrast to the narrator's excessive facility with language. The former communicates with grunts and groans, the latter has a fondness for arcane moods in French grammar. And between them, there is the interlocutor, neither articulate nor inarticulate, merely silent.

The narrator offers to act as translator. He orders gin for the interlocutor. The narrator's gambit, therefore, is to translate between Dutch and French on one level, between bestial

---

1. For a study of the role of silence in Camus, see Laurent MAILHOT, *Albert Camus ou l'imagination du désert* (Montréal, Les Presses de l'Université de Montréal, 1973), chapter XIII, « L'Espace du silence ».

grunts and civilized speech on the other. What is a translator? Simply, a translator is one who transposes a message
from one code to another. The basic presumption of translation is that a message can endure the passage from one
language to the next, that something such as a message
indeed exists which may, in principle, weather the rigours of
passage. Translation consists of three components : the
issuer of the message, the translator who conveys it and the
recipient of the message. The aim of translation is that the
sender and the recipient communicate as if the translator
were not there. The better the translator, the less his presence should enter into the communication. In fact, the translator should strive to minimize his presence ; translation is
best when the translator is not perceived as an active
participant. The ideal translator would be invisible.

This state of affairs becomes more complicated when the
metaphoric identity of the bartender is taken into account.
The narrator does not simply translate from Dutch to French,
but from animalistic grunts to civilized discourse. The
problem, then, is to translate into language what is essentially pre-linguistic. Although they offer no solution, the first
few pages of *La Chute* pose the problem of the passage
into language (of an individual and of the human species).
As we shall see shortly, the bartender's business is not
restricted to doling out drinks (his sideline explains, in some
part, his suspicious nature), but for the moment, let us
simply consider his more legitimate position in *Mexico-City*.

Son métier consiste à recevoir des marins de toutes les nationa-
lités dans ce bar d'Amsterdam qu'il a appelé d'ailleurs, on ne sait
pourquoi, *Mexico-City*. Avec de tels devoirs, on peut craindre, ne
pensez-vous pas, que son ignorance soit inconfortable? Imaginez
l'homme de Cro-Magnon pensionnaire à la tour de
Babel!   (1475)[2]

2. References to quotations from *La Chute* refer to the pagination of
Albert CAMUS, *Théâtre, récits, nouvelles* (Paris, Gallimard, « Bibliothèque
de la Pléiade », 1962 ; 1962 printing).

The bartender holds court over a motley troupe of sailors in Amsterdam. He is described as the Cro-Magnon man lodged in the Tower of Babel. The Tower of Babel has entered our vocabulary as the noun *babel*, "A confusion of sounds, noises, or languages"[3], Babel is noise that may or may not be language. Because it is neither pure noise, nor language in the strict sense, babel is a fitting term to describe the linguistic adventures of the bartender, who himself is half man half animal. It will be remembered that the story of the Tower of Babel appears in Genesis, where man's hybris for building a tower so high that it threatens to pierce the sky is punished by a confusion of tongues. God disciplines man by making communication problematic. Whereas before the Tower of Babel man presumably spoke one language˙ and therefore could communicate freely, after God's chastizement, language became a barrier rather than a bridge. What before had been oneness became multiplicity. The story of the Tower of Babel does not, however, simply allegorize the proliferation of tongues. In fact, God's punishment does not merely create *languages*, but constitutes the notion of *language*. Before there were many languages, it is unlikely that language was evident as such. At most, it was considered natural, an inevitable part of growing up, like growing limbs and sprouting hairs. Once, however, there is not one language, but languages, once communication is not automatic, but a struggle, the artificiality of language becomes apparent. What Saussure called the arbitrariness of the signifier could not appear as such until other signifiers signifying the same signified appeared[4]. The story of the Tower of Babel is an allegorical version of the making arbitrary of the signifier.

It is only when the signifier is arbitrary, that is, when there is more than one language, that two things occur. One, the need for translators arises. Two, nostalgia sets in for that

---

3. *The American Heritage Dictionary of the English Language* (Boston, Houghton Mifflin, 1979), p. 95.
4. Ferdinand de SAUSSURE, *Cours de linguistique générale* (Paris, Payot, 1965 [1915]).

time before translators were needed and as I have stated
previously, the role of the translator becomes to nullify
himself. The Cro-Magnon man, who hardly speaks at all,
presides over a bar he himself names. There are, perhaps,
chinks in his ignorance.

The bar is in Amsterdam and it is frequented by sailors.
Descartes' residence for many years, Amsterdam is a port
city. Like most ports, Amsterdam has a reputation for liveli-
ness bordering on bawdiness. Even though the Dutch are
known for their equilibrium, Amsterdam has a risqué side no
visitor to the city can miss. In fact, ports and various kinds
of laxness go hand in hand. A port, after all, is unique
among cities ; or rather, all the characteristics which define a
city are concentrated in a port. Like all cities, only more so, a
port is a site for exchange. It is a middle ground, a place
where products are not produced or consumed, but through
which they must pass on their trajectory from production to
consumption. Furthermore, a port is frequented by sailors, a
race whose lot it is to roam, whose randiness is perhaps not
the result of their mobility but identical to it. In this port, in
the ambiguous reaches of the waterfront, in a bar which has
been named Mexico-City by the bartender, an as yet
unnamed narrator offers to serve as translator to an unsu-
specting Frenchman[5].

The narrator, therefore, offers to play a role analogous to
that played by the city in which he has chosen to practise
his new career. Just as he would be a translator, a carrier of
meaning, so Amsterdam is a site of exchange. Whether the
product be something sold in the warehouses of Amsterdam
or words exchanged in a sleazy bar, the essential function of
the two, that of a medium of exchange, is identical. Both are
a bridge between producer and consumer and both are
responsible for the integrity of their product as it effects its
passage. Both furthermore, imply distance. Commerce would

---

5. Camus himself visited Amsterdam in October, 1954. For an analysis
of Camus' choice of setting, especially as it relates to Dante's circles of
Hell, see Pierre-Louis REY, Camus : La Chute (Paris, Hatier, 1970).

be unnecessary in a world where goods were produced and consumed in the same place by the same person. Similarly, before God's petulance at the Tower of Babel, translators were unnecessary. Translation, it appears, is simply the linguistic version of exchange in general.

The narrator is quick to point out his dissimilarity to the bartender. Whereas the Cro-Magnon man is inarticulate and distrustful of people, the narrator is talkative and sociable. In fact, his use of language is too skilful. As he points out when his interlocutor smiles at his use of a precious tense, he has a weakness for fine speech[6]:

Quand je vivais en France, je ne pouvais rencontrer un homme d'esprit sans qu'aussitôt j'en fisse ma société. Ah! je vois que vous bronchez sur cet imparfait du subjonctif. J'avoue ma faiblesse pour ce mode, et pour le beau langage, en général. Faiblesse que je me reproche, croyez-le. Je sais bien que le goût du linge fin ne suppose pas forcément qu'on ait les pieds sales. N'empêche. Le style, comme la popeline, dissimule trop souvent de l'eczéma. Je m'en console en me disant qu'après tout, ceux qui bafouillent, non plus, ne sont pas purs.   (1476)

The narrator makes a point of both advertising his penchant for fine speech and questioning the motivations behind it. Verbal facility, he claims, can be a mask, a piece of silk covering eczema[7]. Language, therefore, can lie and since the narrator is apparently a professional talker, he is also, perhaps a professional lier. After their second gin arrives, that is, as the first and second drinks weave their way into the interlocutor's brain and begin to soften his perceptions, the narrator reveals his profession. He is a judge-penitent, formerly a lawyer. Only after he has revealed his profession

---

6. Many critics have noticed Clamence's penchant for fine speech. A particularly helpful analysis, to which I will return, is Jacqueline Lévi-Valensi's, « *La Chute*, ou la parole en procès », *Albert Camus*, n° 3, « Sur *La Chute* », 1970, pp. 33-57.

7. For an extended analysis of the image of the mask as it appears in *La Chute*, see Roger QUILLIOT, « Clamence et son masque », *Ibid.*, pp. 81-100.

does he name himself.

Jean-Baptiste Clamence claims to have practised law, a profession whose major tool is language. Like an artist, a novelist for example, who is said to represent the world, a lawyer represents a client. In both instances representation is occasioned by the muteness of that which is represented. The artist must represent a world which presents itself non-verbally. Similarly, a lawyer speaks for a client who is essentially silent. The client who hires a lawyer is, of course, capable of speech, but in the specific arena of a court of law, he is unable to manipulate the appropriate code. He needs a lawyer to translate his case into a language appropriate to a tribunal. Indeed a lawyer's strength is not necessarily in the evidence he has at his disposal. Evidence is democratic, it is available to all and it is silent. A lawyer's task is not so much to present evidence, but to present it in a certain way. A lawyer is a port. First because he is the intermediary between his client and the court (the judge and/or jury). Second, because he can translate facts or accounts into a code which is understandable in a court. And third, because he need not concern himself with the nature of the products whose conduit he is. Clamence claims that those who have a gift for fine language often use their verbal power to cover truth. A lawyer should, in principle, defend a client without regard for his innocence or guilt. In fact a guilty client poses a greater problem and is therefore a greater challenge for a skilful lawyer. Like those Sophists who so vexed Plato, a lawyer is one who is so adept at manipulating language that he can as easily defend the guilty as the innocent. The truth of a client's guilt or innocence is but one more piece of evidence to be skilfully manipulated by a lawyer whose rhetorical powers are essentially independent of fact. Otherwise, he would not be necessary.

La Chute, then, begins with an encounter. Two kinds of silence, the barely human, visceral sounds of the bartender, reminiscent of the fundamentally silent cacophony of nature and its foil, the literal silence of the interlocutor, stand in sharp contrast to the verbosity of the narrator. These three states, silence, noise and language, are normally assumed to belong to a historical or transcendental progression. Silence gives way to noise which gets organized into language. The movement from silence to language is also the passage from meaninglessness to meaning. And even though meaning or language is always vulnerable to decay into babel, as long as it originates in something which is not itself, it is always, in principle, isolable from its perversions[8]. Perhaps the most powerful philosophical exposition of the transcendental necessity to base language on silence, to ground expression in pre-expression, is Edmund Husserl's phenomenology[9]. Jacques Derrida, in his *La Voix et le phénomène,* deftly demonstrates the logical inconsistencies of such a position at the same time that he refuses to ignore its necessity[10]. The passage from silence to expression is both impossible and a necessary condition of thought. Clamence, who cannot stop speaking, seeks silence ; that is, by his own admission, his narrative is nothing but the protracted attempt to suppress a mocking laugh he encountered one evening on a Paris bridge. Confessing in order to produce silence, Clamence generates a text in which the silence of both the bartender and the interlocutor follows, literally, his own volubility which, in turn, is intended to create the conditions for its eventual annihilation. The chronology suggested here, a chronology which is as necessary in any novel as it is in *Genesis* (where the text of the *Bible* precedes God's logos which subsequently creates silence, animal sounds, human speech and then babel), is, in every sense of the word, unnatural. My analysis of *La Chute* will seek to elucidate the

8. The passage from discourse (*Rede*) to idle talk (*Gerede*) is an essential and unavoidable phenomenon constitutive of Dasein's Being for Heidegger. See chapter 35, "Idle Talk", in *Being and Time* (New York, Harper and Row, 1962), pp. 211-4.

9. See Edmund HUSSERL, *Logical Investigations* (New York, Humanities Press, 1970).

10. *La Voix et le phénomène* (Paris, PUF, 1972).

logic of this deviation in a novel which, after all, is about the absence of God.

THE FALL

CLAMENCE'S monologue is an attempt to silence laughter. The laughter he heard while crossing the Pont des Arts one autumn evening inaugurates his fall. There is no need to summarize here the major movement of the text. I am not suggesting that Clamence's realization of his hypocrisy is unimportant or uninteresting. It is, in fact, the spine of the book. As I noted in the Introduction, I will try as much as possible to refrain from establishing hierarchies of meaning. I will not dwell on Clamence's revelations concerning his former life as a Parisian lawyer and his subsequent realization that it had been a theatrical performance to assure his invulnerability to judgment because it has been done so well by so many others. Brian T. Fitch, for example, in « Une Voix qui se parle, qui nous parle, que nous parlons, ou l'espace théâtral de *La Chute* »[1], explores the theatricality of Clamence's performance : « *Avec la révélation de la fin du livre, tout univers romanesque s'écroule pour ne laisser que la parole de l'acteur.* » (p. 75). Although I will not forget this dominant theme in Clamence's confession, my focus will be elsewhere.

Clamence, a professional of language, was enjoying the silence of Paris one evening :

Il y avait peu de monde sur les quais ; Paris mangeait déjà. Je foulais les feuilles jaunes et poussiéreuses qui rappelaient encore l'été. Le ciel se remplissait peu à peu d'étoiles qu'on apercevait fugitivement en s'éloignant d'un lampadaire vers un autre. Je goûtais le silence revenu, la douceur du soir, Paris vide. J'étais content.   (1492)

---

1. *Albert Camus*, n° 3, « Sur *La Chute* », 1970, pp. 59-79.

Clamence's gaze vacillates between the stars and street lamps. Actually, these two sources of light do not simply follow one another in his perception. The stars are only visible when they are not shrouded by the stronger light emanating from the street lamps. The rhythm established as he strolls along the banks of the Seine is one of obfuscation and manifestation. The lesser, more distant lights from the sky are alternately revealed and hidden as Clamence walks past a series of lamps. There is more to his promenade, however, than competition between two kinds of light. The stars are suns ; they are natural sources of light. The street lamps, on the other hand, are artificial devices. And yet, like the sun during the day, they are able to erase the stars from the sky. Lamps are able to block out the light coming from distant suns. But it is precisely because *the* sun is absent, the sun which is *the* natural source of light, that the street lamps are able to periodically stifle starlight[2]. Street lamps, created by man to compensate for the absent sun, in making vision possible, simultaneously are the occasion for a kind of cecity. As he is caught up in the peculiar rhythm established by two kinds of illumination, Clamence feels a sort of calmness overtaking him. The silence of a deserted Paris is soothing. It does not matter that he is actually in the middle of a modern-day Babel ; for the moment, a warm Paris gloaming allows Clamence the illusion that he is strolling through a deserted city : « § *J'étais monté sur le pont des Arts, désert à cette heure, pour regarder le fleuve qu'on devinait à peine dans la nuit maintenant venue. Face au Vert-Galant, je dominais l'île. Je sentais monter en moi un vaste sentiment de puissance et, comment dirais-je, d'achèvement, qui dilatait mon cœur.* » (1493). As often happens in *La Chute*, Clamence is able to revel in his own

2. The sun has always been the face of a god, invisible because it itself is the source of light. The sun is light, both literal and figurative. For the literal and metaphoric resonances of the sun and especially for its essential filiation to the notion of metaphor, I refer the reader to one of Derrida's most stunning essays, « La Mythologie blanche » in *Marges de la philosophie* (Paris, Editions de Minuit, 1972), pp. 247-307.

potency when he can dominate the landscape from a height[3]. Standing on a bridge named after the arts, he faces an island. It is at this point in the novel, just before he hears the laugh which will precipitate his fall, that a series of images come together to both prefigure what is to come and echo the initial scene in *Mexico-City*. The narrator is recounting a tale to his silent interlocutor about a silent evening in a seemingly deserted Paris. Just before this silence is shattered by a laugh, Clamence is standing on a bridge called Art[4]. He is looking at an island. Since Clamence represents himself as isolated from other people by his narcissism, he is himself an island. Consequently, he is looking at a version of himself from the vantage point of art. And, as I have mentioned previously, since Clamence is a lawyer, another kind of bridge, he is looking at a metaphor of himself from a metaphor of himself. Who, then, is Clamence?

We know what he is not. He is not a real person. He is, at best, the representation of a real person. But to stop there, to see in Clamence the image of reality, would be to ignore his message. His message, quite simply, is that he must keep on speaking to restore the silence he experienced on

3. For an analysis of height and depth from a Bachelardian point of view, see Laurent MAILHOT, *op. cit.*, especially « Chute, gouffre, laby-rinthe », pp. 297-302.

4. A similar structure abounds in *L'Étranger*. Although a case could be made that the laugh in *La Chute* is structurally similar to the ray of light which flies off the Arab's knife and blinds Meursault, or like the numerous other intrusions of a harsh, hot light into Meursault's reveries, the most striking analogy is perhaps with the ship's siren which splits the warm soothing night right before Meursault accepts the mechanical indifference of the universe at the end of the novel : « *Lui parti, j'ai retrouvé le calme. J'étais épuisé et je me suis jeté sur ma couchette. Je crois que j'ai dormi parce que je me suis réveillé avec des étoiles sur le visage. Des bruits de campagne montaient jusqu'à moi. Des odeurs de nuit, de terre et de sel refraîchissaient mes tempes. La merveilleuse paix de cet été endormi entrait en moi comme une marée. À ce moment, et à la limite de la nuit, des sirènes ont hurlé. Elles annonçaient des départs pour un monde qui maintenant m'était à jamais indifférent. Pour la première fois depuis longtemps, j'ai pensé à maman.* » (L'Étranger in *Théâtre, récits, nouvelles*, p. 1209).

the bridge before it was shattered by a laugh. Beyond the content of his monologues, beyond the richness of the auto-biographical tapestry he weaves, lies the inescapable fact of its constant verbal excess. Carina Gadourek, in *Les Innocents et les coupables*[5], argues that Clamence's use of language is primarily a means for the acquisition and mainte-nance of power : « *L'originalité de* La Chute *est de poser le problème de la dictature dans le domaine du langage* [...] *Le langage de Clamence est une arme invincible qui lui assure la toute-puissance.* » (p. 201). For our purposes, let us simply note that Clamence talks to prevent the laugh from re-occurring. His fall, therefore, involves the passage from silence to laughter.

Let us ignore what the laugh means for the moment. Instead, let us focus our attention on the structure of the scene where it is first encountered. The previous passage quoted continues : « *Je me redressai et j'allais allumer une cigarette, la cigarette de la satisfaction, quand, au même moment, un rire éclata derrière moi. Surpris, je fis une brusque volte-face : il n'y avait personne.* » (1493). Novels set up expectations. Fairy tales, for example, make the superna-tural probable. There are no indications in *La Chute* that we are to expect events that are mystical in nature. In fact, several lines later, Clamence qualifies the laugh : « *Entendez-moi bien, ce rire n'avait rien de mystérieux ; c'était un bon rire, naturel, presque amical, qui remettait les choses en place.* » (1493). How, then, are we to understand it. A simple solution would be to attack the text from a psychoanalytic perspective. Such a point of view could yield a conclusion similar to that of Costes who argues that the laugh is actually the exteriorization of Clamence's super-ego:

On a compris que la projection du surmoi sur l'extérieur trouvera un excellent support en la personne du juge. Clamence entendant un éclat de rire sur le pont des Arts l'interprète immé-

5. Carina GADOUREK, *Les Innocents et les coupables. Essai d'ex-égèse de l'œuvre d'Albert Camus* (The Hague, Mouton, 1963).

diatement comme une moquerie. Cette interprétation ne provient que de lui : il a en fait entendu son Surmoi (la voix de sa conscience!), mais *comme venant de l'extérieur*[6].

This is plausible, inasmuch as the simplest explanation of the laugh's meaning would entail a discussion of Clamence's realization of his previous bad faith. But such an interpretation would make of Clamence a hysteric and although it is certainly possible to analyze the novel in this manner, it would violate the rules of reading I outlined earlier. We are left with the following dilemma : a laugh appears *ex nihilo* and yet it cannot be explained as either a supernatural event or a hysterical symptom.

Is it a metaphor then? Yes and no. No, if by metaphor is meant the vehicle for some deep meaning. Yes, if we take the word metaphor literally. Metaphor means the transference of meaning from one signifier to another. It comes from the Greek, μεταφορά, transference. A metaphor, then, is not so much a word as it is a relation. Specifically, a metaphor involves the transfer of a word's literal meaning, to another, figurative, meaning. The site for a transfer of meaning, a metaphor is a linguistic port. A lawyer and a translator, Clamence is himself the vehicle for a certain transport of meaning. In other words, if we define metaphor as the encounter between the literal and figurative functions of language, then when Clamence mediates between silence and self-consciously literary language, he is narrating a novel which postulates its narrator as figuring the passage between pre-predication and metaphoricity.

Clamence's spirits are a direct reflection of the kind of metaphor he imagines himself to be. At moments of manic elation, Clamence feels that he is *sui generis*. Whether he is on a mountain, on the top deck of a ship, or contemplating an island, Clamence feels most potent when he can dominate his environment and therefore feel self-contained. At such moments, Clamence gloats with all the self-possession

6. *Op. cit.*, p. 34.

of one who fantasizes that his vision can saturate his environment while remaining transparent to itself. Bounded by nothing save his self-consciousness, Clamence feels dominant because he imagines himself either as the silence of a pre-linguistic world or as language for which the passage to metaphoricity is a provisional detour of sense out of itself within the horizon of its ultimate reabsorption into the simplicity of the literal. When Clamence imagines himself as an island, he is dreaming of the silence inherent in a perfect equilibrium between language and the world. He feels himself in a position to control both his surroundings and himself because the language he would deploy is capable of subsuming its object with no remainder.

His fall, therefore, is not literally spatial, that is, from height to depth. Or rather, the spatial dimension of his fall is itself a species of a larger genus. Clamence's fall is basically a lapse of vision. The uninterrupted vision afforded by a niche in an aerie, or, at the limit, the fantasied capacity to see not only one's surroundings but also one's vantage point, as when Clamence looks across the Seine at an island which on some level he imagines himself to be, is denatured by an internal blindness. If, as Derrida argues in « La Mythologie blanche », literality is always associated with the proximity and punctuality of vision, then Clamence falls when he encounters within himself a kind of figurative energy resistant to naturalization by exposure to light. Like the rhythmic alternation between lamplight and starlight occasioned not only by Clamence's stroll but by the absence of the sun, Clamence's fall is from a silent perspective where vision has infinite scope to a verbalization or metaphorization of vision. Another way of saying the same thing : when vision passes from a literal, biological function, into a metaphoric state which is essentially catachretic, that is, when the sun is posited as a textual phenomenon, the precipitate is a sarcastic laugh[7].

7. Catachresis, a curious kind of metaphor which serves to designate a thing bereft of a literal name, offers, for Derrida, privileged access to

The laugh is neither hysterical nor mystical. Either explanation of the laugh's presence in *La Chute* seeks ultimately to reinstate the novel within a traditional representational grid. Clearly to see the laugh as a psychological phenomenon would be to seek to explain it through recourse to the psychic depth of Clamence. It is perhaps less obvious why a supernatural explanation does the same thing. The critic would need to demonstrate the supernatural origin of the laugh only if he were interested in maintaining a diacritical difference between it and the rest of the novel. I choose neither path. The laugh is a real laugh which comes from nowhere. Consequently, it cannot be a real laugh. If it is neither real nor unreal, but both, it must be the tension, the tense relation between the two. Like a catachresis, which names a thing and stands as evidence of its lack of a name, the laugh is a crack in the strange alliance between vision and silence.

As Clamence looks around to see where the laugh is coming from, his gaze is diverted from the island :

J'allai jusqu'au garde-fou : aucune péniche, aucune barque. Je me retournai vers l'île et, de nouveau, j'entendis le rire dans mon dos, un peu plus lointain, comme s'il descendait le fleuve. Je restais là, immobile. Le rire décroissait, mais je l'entendais encore distinctement derrière moi, venu de nulle part, sinon des eaux.

(1493)

From the island, his vision is diverted to the river. A bit later, in his bathroom, as he reaches for a glass of water, he notices that his reflection is smiling in the mirror, « *[...] mais il me sembla que mon sourire était double [...]*» (1493). From islands and heights to rivers, water and mirrors ; from single-ness to doubleness ; in short, from stability to passage, that

the figurative tension internal to the constitution of propriety in general. In « La Mythologie blanche », he says : « *Ce qui nous intéresse ici, c'est donc cette production d'un sens propre, d'une nouvelle sorte de sens propre, par la violence d'un catachrèse dont le statut intérmédiaire tend à échapper à l'opposition du primitif et du figuré, tenant entre eux le 'milieu'.* » (pp. 305-6).

is how Clamence describes his fall.

The meaning of the novel's title is overdetermined. The various kinds of falls described in the novel range from the literal (the girl who supposedly committed suicide) to the figurative (Clamence's fall from innocence to guilt, or from hypocrisy to lucidity). Clearly, however, the dominant resonance of the novel's title is of the fall in Genesis. Even though one need not stray from the text to make the analogy between Clamence's confession and the biblical fall, since *La Chute* makes numerous references to Eden, to Christ, to Hell, to the Final Judgment etc. (for example, « *Les juges punissaient, les accusés expiaient et moi, libre de tout devoir, soustrait au jugement comme à la sanction, je régnais, librement, dans une lumière édénique.* » [1487]), its title alone is sufficient to evoke the fate of Adam and Eve. Adam and Eve's punishment for having transgressed God's prohibition is a spatial displacement : they are expelled from Eden. Having been evicted, they begin the human race's single journey : whether it roams in search of the promised land, as in the *Old Testament*, or whether it awaits redemption and a return to paradise, as in the *New Testament*, its trajectory is the same. The human race, exiled from its home, sees its life as the tortuous return to its point of origin. In the Judeo-Christian tradition, the life of a human being is a bridge, between a source and a destination which is essentially similar to the source. In the *New Testament*, the figure of Christ, half human, half divine, represents the passage between exiled mankind and its return to its divine origins.

Like the biblical fall, a fall in general, implies a certain journey. A fall must be a fall from, therefore it contains within itself the notion of an origin and a fall to, implying a destination. In addition, like the biblical fall, the general notion of falling has ethical ramifications. Satan, in the *Bible,* or in his later manifestation in Milton, is a fallen angel. Heidegger, in his ontological analysis of Dasein, labels as falleness the state in which Dasein often finds itself when it disregards its

Being and loses itself in commerce with things[8]. These are but two examples of what needs none. A fall is always a spatial displacement with negative moral implications. Whether a fall is seen as punishment for disobedience, or as a structural part of one's being, it is always constituted by three moments : an original state, a passage and a fallen state[9]. Furthermore, the notion of a fall implies a rebound. To fall is also to be capable of a return.

Clearly, the central fall in *La Chute* is Clamence's into guilt. The vehicle for that fall, the event which precipitates his fall, is itself a fall. Although the novel is studded with falls, the one which stands in the middle of Clamence's confession is that of the young woman.

If we are to believe Clamence, the story of the woman's suicide has structured his monologue : « *Il me semble en tout cas que ce sentiment ne m'a plus quitté depuis cette aventure que j'ai trouvée au centre de ma mémoire et dont je ne peux différer plus longtemps le récit, malgré mes digressions et les efforts d'une invention à laquelle, je l'espère, vous rendez justice.* » (1508). The entirety of Clamence's monologue to this point has been the attempt to defer relating the

---

8. He calls it the "falling" of Dasein (*Verfallen*). See section 38, "Falling and Throwness" in *Being and Time*, pp. 219-24.

9. Heidegger is not as simplistic as this schema might suggest. In fact, he says, "*So neither must we take the falleness of Dasein as a 'fall' from a purer and higher 'primal status'.* » (*Being and Time*, p. 220). Dasein's fall is not from an earlier, pure, state, but from itself. Dasein falls into the world, which is an essential component of its Being. As such, Dasein is always falling. I would suggest, however, that despite Heidegger's care, it is impossible to remove the notion of falling from the metaphorics of exile. Once again, Derrida is trenchant : « *La limite métaphysique ou onto-théléologique consiste sans doute moins à penser une chute dans le temps (depuis un non-temps ou une éternité in-temporelle qui n'a aucun sens chez Hegel), mais à penser une chute en général, fût-ce, comme le propose Sein und Zeit en son thème fondamental et en son lieu de plus grande insistance, d'un temps originaire en un temps dérivé [...] Or l'opposition de l'originaire et du dérivé n'est-elle pas encore métaphysique ? Le [sic] requête de l'archie en général, quelles que soient les précautions dont on entoure ce concept, n'est-elle pas l'opération 'essentielle' de la métaphysique ?* » (« Ousia et Grammè » in *Marges*, pp. 73-4).

story which is about to follow. However, since Clamence is given to exaggeration, it is conceivable that the opposite is true, that the narrative leading up to this pasage is not so much a digression or even an introduction to the central event soon to be recounted, but an essential part of it. At any rate, during the night in question, Clamence was returning home after having been with a mistress. It was drizzling as he approached the pont Royal : « *Sur le pont, je passai derrière une forme penchée sur le parapet, et qui semblait regarder le fleuve. De plus près, je distinguai une mince jeune femme, habillée de noir. Entre les cheveux sombres et le col du manteau, on voyait seulement une nuque, fraîche et mouillée, à laquelle je fus sensible.* » (1509). As opposed to the scene at the pont des Arts, this time Clamence is not alone. He is moved by a young woman dressed in black. His attention to detail suggests that his stare is at least as intense as hers. As intrigued as he is by her, he hesitates only for a moment.

Mais je poursuivis ma route, après une hésitation. Au bout du pont, je pris les quais en direction de Saint-Michel, où je demeurais. J'avais déjà parcouru une cinquantaine de mètres à peu près, lorsque j'entendis le bruit, qui malgré la distance, me parut formidable dans le silence nocturne, d'un corps qui s'abat sur l'eau. Je m'arrêtai net, mais sans me retourner. Presque aussitôt, j'entendis un cri, plusieurs fois répété, qui descendait lui aussi le fleuve, puis s'éteignit brusquement.   (1509)

Once again, silence is shattered by a sound. Unlike the laughter he heard on the pont des Arts, however, this sound is not of mysterious origin. Clamence assumes it to be the sound of a body falling into the Seine. The repeated cries drifting downstream confirm his suspicion that the sound he heard was the splash of the young woman committing suicide. It is important to note, however, that although Clamence was careful in scrutinizing the woman's neck while she was still on the bridge, he does not actually see her jump (or fall) into the river. The text makes it clear that she

does, but it is also equally unequivocal about the nature of
the evidence Clamence uses to reach that conclusion. He
does not see the woman plunge into the dark water ; he
simply hears her striking the river. No sooner does he hear
the initial sound which rends the midnight silence than a
series of cries leaves no doubt as to what had just occurred.

Having done nothing to help the woman in black,
Clamence goes home. For the next couple of days he will
not read the newspaper. The girl's fall is also his fall. So
much goes without saying[10]. But it is not the girl's fall *per
se* which inaugurates Clamence's demise. Although the
woman's fate is clear, Clamence's narrative suggests that
the event of her fall was itself not perceived by Clamence.
Her fall is assumed to have occurred through subsequent
auditory evidence. In fact, her fall is reconstructed. Even
though a body must first fall for the sound of its impact on
the river to be produced and even though the woman must
first be in the river for her to begin emitting cries,
Clamence's monologue reverses this chronology. What must
have happened first, the event, is, in the text, presented
second. Furthermore, the kind of evidence historically
required to verify an event's occurrence, visual evidence, is,
in the case in question, missing[11]. It has been replaced by
what would logically follow it. In fact, the "reality" of the girl's
suicide is produced by what should have been produced by
it.

10. Perhaps not quite. Other critics have seen more in her fall than I
choose to. Jean Gassin, for example, in *L'Univers symbolique d'Albert
Camus* (Paris, Minard, 1981), argues that the girl is actually a displacement of Clamence's mother. In fact, for Gassin, *La Chute* is ultimately a
symbolic matricide.

11. As Derrida has argued, the formulation "visual evidence" is
oxymoronic. Evidence has always been judged by its proximity to visual
proof. Evidence is presence, the immediate (visual) access to an object.
Derrida sees Husserl's "*principle of principles*" (no. 24 in *Ideen*) as an
exemplary formulation of the metaphysical identity between evidence and
presence : « *[...] son* [Husserl's] *'principe des principes' (selon nous son
principe* métaphysique : l'évidence originaire *et la* présence *de la chose
elle-même en personne) [...]*» (« Genèse et Structure » in *L'Écriture et la
différence* [Paris, Seuil, 1967], p. 244).

The scene in which a young woman falls literally and Clamence falls figuratively is itself a figure. As I argued earlier, a metaphor is the transfer of a signifier from a literal to figurative signified. The point of a metaphor, in most rhetorics, is that comparison with a concrete meaning is useful in delimiting or somehow making more palpable an abstract one. The assumption of such a comparison is that a concrete signified is accessible in an unproblematic way. If I compare the state to a ship, I am illustrating a complex, intangible, entity, by comparison with a corporeal object. That is, something which can be seen, if only in the mind's eye, will clarify, or make visible, what is essentially invisible. The basic structural element of the metaphor, the transfer of meaning from a concrete signified to an abstract one, are present in the scene under discussion. The woman's plunge simultaneously occasions and illustrates Clamence's. However, unlike the traditional dynamics of the metaphor, the central scene in *La Chute* pieces together the concrete event from subsequent clues. Let me repeat : I am not suggesting that the narrative questions in any way that the girl fell into the river. I am simply pointing out that her fall is never perceived, but reconstructed from clues. Although I am not yet ready to make that claim, it is perhaps beginning to appear that Clamence's fear of bridges does not stem from the woman's fall, but from a bridge's participation in a curious relation between the literal and the figurative. However, for the moment, let us refrain from hasty judgments and restrict ourselves to the following observations:

A bridge joins two pieces of land. If there were not a rift, in the form of a river in this instance, a bridge would be unnecessary. In connecting, a bridge points to the space it spans. Like the translator, who, after one of mankind's many falls, makes communication possible to the extent that he assures that it will never be complete, a bridge both joins two shores and indicates the cleft between them. Furthermore, both bridges and translators imply a certain vector. A bridge allows one to go from one shore to another.

Implicit in such a passage is the existence of a place of origin and a destination. Before a bridge can become think- able, that is, before it can perform its function of synthesis and alienation, there must be a river and two shores. Before a message can set out on its journey via the intermediary of a translator, there must be an emitter and a recipient. And before one can fall, the world must afford at least two places.

Thus far I have culled from *La Chute* five varieties of passage. Three are clearly kinds of falls : the literal fall of the young woman into the Seine, the fall of Adam and Eve and the fall of humanity into a multitude of languages. Two exploit the metaphorics of connection : the notions of trans- lation and legal representation. Although the second group appears to function horizontally, it is clearly related to the first group. A translator is only required if there is plurality of human tongues and a lawyer's services imply the possibility of guilt. On the simplest level, then, *La Chute* would appear to deploy a series of variants of its title. Needless to say, the most popular interpretation of the novel, involving Clamence's fall from hypocrisy to lucidity, fits squarely into this model. Although the five kinds of transition are distinct and should not be confused, they share a basic isomorphism. They all assume that passage is between two points which predate the passage. This supposition is clear in the case of a literal fall. A thing falls from somewhere to somewhere else. Similarly, in the story of the fall in *Genesis*, Adam and Eve first find themselves in a place which preceded them. In fact, since they had never had another home, it is unlikely that the idea of another place would have been thinkable to them. It is from this home, from this property which was proper to them, that they are banished. Analogously, the story of the Tower of Babel assumes that before God's pique, humanity spoke one tongue. The point of origin, then, was linguistic homogeneity. God's punishment, the degeneration of the universal tongue into babel, is to make communication into a problematic activity. Translation and law are essentially postlapsarian professions. They are only necessary after the fall from grace and the fall from linguistic unity.

The structures of passage on which I have focused, a metaphor for which is the metaphor, are similar in assuming an origin and a destination. Whether the destination is another place, or merely the point of departure, the structure is identical in that it presumes that passage requires the pre-existence of a source and a telos. Such, at least, is the traditional meaning of passage[12].

12. I use the term "traditional" advisedly. It frequently connotes something belonging to the unenlightened past and which some incisive contemporary methodology will disrupt. Although, of course, there is an element of that kind of arrogance in my discourse, I wish to make the following point as clear as possible : meaning is always traditional. The meaning which accrues to a term is historically and culturally determined and as such is contained within the term. As I argue in my introduction, a basic premise of this analysis is that meaning is not layered. I should now explain myself a bit further. I do not think that a text has an unconscious. That is, I don't believe that one layer of meaning masks another. I do, however, concede that certain meanings are dominant. Words are necessarily traditional. They mean in certain fixed ways ; consequently, they mean hierarchically. Furthermore, in the microcontext of a literary work (as opposed to the macrocontext of a culture), words interact to produce meaning which is often at odds with the ways they normally produce meaning. Am I contradicting myself? How can several meanings entertain a hierarchical relation in a text which is nevertheless not deployed in layers? The answer is that although microcontextual and macrocontextual meanings coexist in a text and although they are often at odds with each other, their relation exists in a single dimension. An example might help : suppose that in a certain novel, signifier R (rose, river etc.) abounds. Furthermore, it is clear that from its deployment in the text, that R comes to acquire a different denotation than that which traditionally accrues to it. In addition, let us suppose that three of four additional denotations get attached to R in the same text. These supplementary denotations, all different from the traditional and microcontextual connotations and denotations of R, appear in the text with less emphasis. They are mentioned with less insistence, or only sporadically, etc. Clearly we have a hierarchy. But, do we have layers? Are we authorized to claim that meaning (in the large sense, including the traditional concepts of connotation, denotation etc.) A is a mask hiding meaning B, which itself somehow conceals meaning C etc. Such a model, which is essentially Freudian, implicitly makes an analogy between a text and the model for the human mind posited by psychoanalysis. (The relation between literary criticism and psychoanalysis is complex. An excellent study of the gamut of psychoanalytically based approaches to

Clamence's spiritual fall is occasioned by a literal fall. His inaction when he imagines a young woman to have jumped or fallen into the Seine precipitates the realization that his former life as a Parisian lawyer had been a sham. The remainder of the novel will be a description and an illustration of Clamence's ruse to circumvent the acceptance of his guilt. My analysis of Clamence's resistance to guilt will be guided not so much by a catalogue of ideas culled from Clamence's monologue, but by its textual dynamics. Clamence's realization of his guilt and his adoption of the profession of judge-penitent do not occur in a vacuum. Jean-Baptiste Clamence's baptism in guilt is not a real event which the novel is describing any more than Clamence is a real person. I am stating the obvious, but it is easily forgotten. Clamence is a fictional character and all we know of him and his plight is what can be culled from his monologue. There is no story preceding his monologue to which it can be compared for accuracy.

The novel inscribes the received notion of a fall in a specific way. That is, the literariness of *La Chute* does not depend on the story it tells, but on the text's structure as it organizes and articulates the telling of its story. It is

the study of literary texts is *Psychanalyse et littérature* [Paris, PUF, 1978] by Jean Bellemin-Noël. See also, from the same author, *Vers l'inconscient du texte : « Écriture »* [Paris, PUF, 1978].) Whatever one's position towards psychoanalysis as a philosophical or therapeutic praxis, I think it is presumptious to make of a literary text a wounded being, cloaking some meanings and revealing others. R, in our example, means differently at different places in the text and some of its meanings are incompatible. All of them, however, are present and available with disconcerting simplicity.

The notion of a fall comes to *La Chute* already belonging to a philosophical and theological tradition. The text uses these received meanings ; it confirms some and disrupts others. The remainder of this study will be an attempt to demonstrate how *La Chute* re-transcribes the idea of a fall. The evidence I will offer will not be the result of critical legerdemain. By no means will I seek to "deconstruct" the book. On the contrary, my goal is to show how the book creates the possiblity for thinking something like deconstruction in general. (For the best work ever done on the auto-deconstructive nature of literature, see : Paul DE MAN, *Blindness and Insight* [New York, Oxford University Press, 1971].)

precisely this articulation which will hold our attention. In the first chapter, soon after Clamence has compared Amsterdam's canals to the circles of Hell, he leaves his companion at the threshold of a bridge:

> À demain donc, monsieur et cher compatriote. Non, vous trouverez maintenant votre chemin ; je vous quitte près de ce pont. Je ne passe jamais sur un pont, la nuit. C'est la conséquence d'un vœu. Supposez, après tout, que quelqu'un se jette à l'eau. De deux choses l'une, ou vous l'y suivez pour le repêcher et, dans la saison froide, vous risquez le pire! Ou vous l'y abandonnez et les plongeons rentrés laissent parfois d'étranges courbatures. (1481)

At this early point in the narrative, Clamence's adumbration of his encounter with the young woman in black goes unnoticed. At best, it is read as a whimsical, meaning-laden, image. The attentive reader will notice, for example, the structural similarity between translation, law, a port and a bridge. The reference of Clamence's foreshadowing, however, is as yet unknown.

Just as the first chapter ends with a cryptic reference to the role bridges are to play in Clamence's story, the second chapter is brought to a close by the laughter scene. On the pont des Arts, Clamence heard a laugh which was to haunt him. I have already mentioned that the internal structure of this scene is dominated by the relation of sound to silence. I will return to that idea shortly. For now, however, let us simply notice that this scene, whose position at the end of chapter two is analogous to Clamence's first mention of his bridge phobia at the end of chapter one, precedes the climactic scene at the pont Royal by a chapter. The latter scene, at the end of chapter three, is both at the heart of Clamence's memory and in the approximate centre of *La Chute*. The event described during this scene, the possible death of a young woman, is the origin of Clamence's fall. The laughter of the preceding scene is clearly related to Clamence's inaction on the pont Royal. The relation is one of cause to effect. Whatever our interpretation of the laugh, it is impossible to ignore the mocking commentary it makes on Clamence's cowardice. However, in addition to that legitimate reading of these two scenes, which makes of them a moment of Existentialist illumination, there is another, simpler, use to which they can be put.

Various linguists and critics have defined the terms "narrative" and "plot" in a number of ways. For the purposes of this analysis, I shall define these terms as follows : plot is the story whereas narrative is the telling of the story. In the case of the three scenes in question, their chronology in the narrative is : At the end of chapter one, Clamence mentions an as yet unexplained fear of bridges. At the end of chapter two, he describes the laugh he heard on the pont des Arts. At the end of chapter three, the young woman's plunge explains the previous two scenes. The chronology of the three scenes in the plot is not the same. The first mention of bridges occurs in the present of the narrative. The laughter scene, which in the narrative precedes the fall scene, in the plot follows it by several years : « *Cette nuit-là, en novembre, deux ou trois ans avant le soir où je crus entendre rire dans mon dos, je regagnais la rive gauche, et mon domicile, par le pont Royal.* » (1509). The text, therefore, inverts the order of the plot. What in the plot occurred second appears first in the narrative.

When did Clamence's fall occur? The plot of the novel produces the following sequence : 1. He fails to assist a young woman whom he suspects to have fallen into the Seine. Her literal fall, therefore, inaugurates his figurative one. 2. Several years later, while crossing another Paris bridge, he hears a laugh which merely reinforces the earlier event. 3. Finally, some time after he heard the laugh, Clamence spots a piece of jetsam on the ocean while entertaining a female friend on board an ocean liner. The black speck recalls the young woman, also clad in black. Clamence's fall is complete:

Je compris alors, sans révolte, comme on se résigne à une idée dont on connaît depuis longtemps la vérité, que ce cri qui, des années auparavant, avait retenti sur la Seine, derrière moi, n'avait pas cessé, porté par le fleuve vers les eaux de la Manche, de cheminer dans le monde, à travers l'étendue illimitée de l'océan, et qu'il m'y avait attendu jusqu'à ce jour où je l'avais rencontré.   (1529)

The narrative reverses the order of the laugh and the suicide scenes. It could, of course, be argued that the order of presentation of these scenes is simply a stylistic flourish on the part of Camus, that he thought that his point could be made more poignantly if he reversed the expected sequence. Such arguments are, I think, speculative. My only source of evidence is the text of *La Chute*, so it is only to Clamence's confession that I have recourse.

The text offers some indications of the motive behind its narrative sequence. Briefly, the order in which *La Chute* presents the scenes under consideration is the answer to the question concerning the origin of Clamence's fall. The answer is complex. It involves what Freud calls *Nachträglichkeit*[13]. Although Clamence's fall was certainly caused by his hesitation on the pont Royal, the meaning of that event lay latent until the laughter scene. Clamence admits to an extraordinary ability to forget. Whether we call his forgetfulness, repression, bad faith, etc. is secondary, I think, to its function in the narrative. The concrete effect of Clamence's talent is to allow him to continue his life in the two or three years between the suicide and the laughter as if the girl had never fallen into the river. The previously cited passage preceding Clamence's encounter with the laugh attests to the heights of narcissistic self-satisfaction he had managed to reach following the pont Royal scene. Although

13. This is Freud's theory of deferred action. References to it are common in Freud's work. See, for example, Standard Edition (*Complete Psychological Works of Sigmund Freud*, ed. James Strachey [London, Hogarth Press, 1954]), XVII, 45, no. 1, III, p. 167 ; and *The Origins of Psychoanalysis*, ed. Anna Freud, Marie Bonaparte and Ernst Kris (New York, Basic Books, 1954), Part II, pp. 410-3

Clamence claims to have forgotten the laugh a few days after he heard it, both by his own admission and through textual evidence, it would appear that his life suffered irreparable change following its irruption on the pont des Arts. Clamence himself explains : « § *Avec quelques autres vérités, j'ai découvert ces évidences peu à peu, dans la période qui suivit le soir dont je vous ai parlé. Pas tout de suite, non, ni très distinctement. Il a fallu d'abord qui je retrouve ma mémoire. Par degrés, j'ai vu plus clair, j'ai appris un peu de ce que je savais.* » (1498). In fact, chapter three is manifestly different from the two previous chapters. The first chapter functions as an introduction both of Clamence to his interlocutor and of the various narrative and thematic structures of the book to the reader. Chapter two describes the pinnacles of hypocrisy Clamence had reached during his law career in Paris. Following the laughter scene, at the end of chapter two, the book begins its descent. Chapter three, describing as it does Clamence's views on slavery, the incident with the motorcyclist and Clamence's relationships with women, is decidedly downbeat. By the end of chapter three, with its crucial and climactic pont Royal scene, the fall, which the woman's suicide in principle inaugurates, is well under way.

The text, therefore, although it reverses the chronology of the events it recounts, presents an accurate representation of the genesis of Clamence's fall. As opposed to the traditional meaning of a fall, a meaning which, as I have noted earlier, is inscribed in the word *fall* and is impossible to ignore, *La Chute* offers a fall which functions according to a different logic. The narrative and the plot of the novel conspire to retranscribe the temporal and spatial configuration of the received notion of a fall.

A fall implies a certain metaphysics of time and space. The idea of a fall is normally thinkable as the passage from an original position of innocence to a subsequent state of guilt. It therefore conjoins the temporal idea of a beginning, transition and end, with the spatial notion of descent from one place to another. In fact, the idea of a beginning is the temporal equivalent of the idea of the point from which the fall begins. Ethical, spatial, temporal and metaphysical presuppositions converge in the concept of a fall in a way that has been powerfully overdetermined in our culture. It is precisely this concatenation of metaphysical axioms which *La Chute* disrupts. I am, of course, not making any claims as to the effect of the novel's microcontext on the macrocontext which we call the world. Their relation is far more complex than any relation of cause and effect. In fact, it is just such a relation that the novel is taking to task.

There is no simple answer to the question concerning the origin of Clamence's fall. Although his fall began the day he scurried home having failed to come to the aid of the woman in black, this beginning remained latent until he heard the laughter on the pont des Arts several years later. His fall, therefore, begins properly with the second event. What comes second precedes what comes first. And, since the cause of the laugh is clearly the event which is described as having occurred earlier, the text presents a paradoxical sequence of causality in which the result engenders the cause. And the narrative, as if to demonstrate that the logic it maintains is the logic of its own textuality, offers first what its own plot maintains happened second and vice versa.

I shall discuss the implications of this reversal later. For now, let me simply emphasize the radical disruption of the notions or origin and point of origin it effects. The question asked earlier concerning the origin of Clamence's fall, whose very form makes it one of the seminal questions of philosophy, is inadequate to the novel. To ask the question, "When?", a question in which is inscribed the form of an answer, is to assume that events begin and end. As long as the beginning of Clamence's fall can be described, as long as a beginning can be said to have occurred, then the trajectory of his fall is in principle traceable. The integrity of a passage can be safeguarded only if its origin and its destination are delimitable. Therefore, especially in the circular case where the end is the beginning, the very thinkability of a fall and of its subsequent recuperation via a return to the origin depends on the possibility of a discrete beginning[14]. *La Chute*, whose title leads the reader to expect it to be a variant of the classic fall story, is actually the story of a fall whose origin is dispersed. It is a novel positing the impossibility of a first time.

A problem appears to have arisen in my analysis. Although I admit the possibility of coexistence between traditional meanings and those created by a literary text, the tone and direction of my reading imply that a distinction must be made between different microcontextual meanings. Although it is not within the province of this analysis to enter into the labyrinthian problem of the mechanics of a text's production of sense, it is arguable that meaning results from the encounter of three elements : the text (words, syntax, punctuation, spacing, paper quality, etc.), the meanings the culture gives the text and the way those meanings are transformed and/or deformed by an individual reader. "The novel" is the precipitate of this encounter. It does not exist outside of it. Consequently, any variation in one, two or three of its components changes the meaning of a text. In the case under consideration, the same text with the same (relatively) cultural context means differently because the third element constitutive of its meaning is by definition biased in unpredictable ways. Specifically, I maintain that my analysis of *La Chute* is not only at variance with certain culturally determined modes of conceptualization, but also with traditional interpretations of the text. For example, a common reading of the novel, such as Jean-Claude Brisville's – « 'Prophète vide pour temps médiocre', *dit Clamence de lui-même, et il suffit déjà pour le connaître de savoir entendre*

---

14. It is possible to argue that all journeys aspire to just such a configuration. No one has better elucidated the relation between origin and telos than Derrida. It would be possible, following Derrida, to define the concept of Western Metaphysics as the essential identity between the originating logos and the eschatos. See, among other places, *L'Origine de la géométrie*, translation (of Husserl's text) and introduction by Jacques Derrida (Paris, PUF, Coll. « Epiméthée », 1962).

*son nom, Jean-Baptiste... Le Précurseur. Clamence... la voix
dans le désert. Mais cette voix n'annonce rien, si ce n'est la
culpabilité générale.* »[15] – maintains that Camus' Existential
message is that all of humanity is essentially guilty ; in a
universe without God, the notion of innocence is meaning-
less, consequently all that is available to man are various
degrees of guilt. I do not dispute such an interpretation. On
the contrary, I think it is accurate and explains much of
Clamence's monologue. The reason for this analysis is
neither to repeat previous interpretations nor to refute them. I
only mean to add to them. Although I agree that the gener-
alization of guilt to include all of mankind and the bracketting
of the notion of innocence are meanings produced by the
text, I think *La Chute* is actually more subversive than that.
Even if the Judeo-Christian notion of original guilt is radical-
ized to the extent that it includes Adam from the moment of
his creation, that is, even if innocence were rendered an
impossible state for man, as long as guilt continues to function within a necessarily Judeo-Christian context, it will still
maintain a diacritical relation to innocence. The fact that
innocence is unattainable because it never existed in no way
denatures its pervasiveness. In fact, the traditional reading of
La Chute cannot help but see alongside Clamence's merci-
less condemnation of mankind a relatively undisguised
nostalgia for that period in his life when he imagined himself
innocent. For example, in a section of the third chapter of his
book on *La Chute* entitled « La Nostalgie de l'absolu »[16],
Pierre-Louis Rey claims that Clamence's concession is a
compensation for an Eden he discovers to be inaccessible :
« *Aussi insaississable soit-elle, nous inclinerions volontiers à
penser que l'attitude humoristique et provocante de
Clamence trouve sa source dans une nostalgie profonde de
l'absolu.* » The profession of judge-penitent, at least as he
describes it to his interlocutor, is nothing else than an elabo-

---

15. Jean-Claude BRISVILLE, *Camus* (Paris, Gallimard, coll.
« Bibliothèque idéale », 1959), pp. 76-7.
16. Pierre-Louis REY, *Camus* : La Chute, p. 57.

rate ruse to reinstate Clamence in his Eden. Eden, for Clamence, is freedom from judgment : « *Les juges punissaient, les accusés expiaient et moi, libre de tout devoir, soustrait au jugement comme à la sanction, je régnais, librement, dans une lumière édénique.* » (1487). Eden is light, it is a kind of baptism which, unlike Clamence's other baptism, promises a certain kind of freedom. Specifically, Eden, inasmuch as it predates the idea of judgement, suspends the possibility of guilt. On a certain level, Clamence never ceases searching for that light. To universalize guilt, consequently, can result in an obsession with innocence. The etymology of *metaphysics* attests elegantly to man's refusal to abandon the search for the unattainable simply because it is beyond his reach. In fact, inaccessibility is also inviolability. Since it would be catastrophic to find innocence only to discover that it is tainted, man has resorted to the deceptively simple stratagem of situating it on a plane juridically removed from the here and now. Whether we call it childhood, a state of grace, the state of nature, etc., the notion of innocence thrives on distance. To maintain that all humanity is guilty is not in principle different from the Christian version of the same claim. And if innocence is, as Clamence says, no longer a possibility for modern man, it is still a presence, albeit at a remove, structuring his life. The brand of Existentialism traditionally associated with Camus (which typically arises from the imposition of *Le Mythe de Sisyphe* onto his novels), in which man must struggle against his own nostalgia for God in an indifferent universe, is essentially negative theology. If by removing God one creates a hole, an absence which serves the same fundamental purpose as God, then not much has changed. Separated from innocence, guilty beyond reprieve, man is still in the sway of the couplet guilt/innocence.

There is much in *La Chute* to support such an interpretation. I am not suggesting that my refusal to admit of levels excludes the possibility of a certain multiplicity. In fact, I contend that to see a literary text deployed in strata is, paradoxically, to reduce it. *La Chute* is multiple, in part, because it invites a range of interpretations. I am suggesting that whereas the test does not exclude a traditional Existentialist interpretation, it also invites another kind of reading. At the same time that Clamence is stuck in the quagmire of the massively metaphysical opposition between guilt and innocence, he is narrating a text which suggests the possibility of another kind of logic.

The passage cited above continues, in a new paragraph : « § *N'était-ce pas cela, en effet, l'Eden, cher monsieur : la vie en prise directe?* » (1487).

THE JUST JUDGES

LA CHUTE is a confession. It follows in the line of such familiar confessions as those of Augustine and Rousseau. And although these are supposedly non-fiction, while *La Chute* is clearly fictional, their structure is similar in many respects. Whether a confession purports to tell a "true" story or whether it narrates a fiction which it presents as true is of little consequence. The structuring element of a confession is that it is a narrative which seeks to baptise its narrator. The classic confession, that of Augustine, for example, is written from the perspective of a narrator who, having been saved, is able to narrate the story of his fall into depravity from the safe haven of his conversion. *La Chute* could have fitted into the same schema. Of course, the signs would have to have been changed. Clamence's monologue would be a negative confession which, instead of seeking to demonstrate the innocence of the narrator, strives to prove that not only is he guilty, but that all of humanity is equally guilty. *La Chute* would have been such a confession if it did not thematize its own narration.

In its traditional manifestation, a confession is an admission of some truth. If *La Chute* were a simple confession, the truth structuring it would be Clamence's realization of his guilt when he did not run to the aid of a young woman who, he supposed, jumped into the Seine. However, as I have already suggested, the truth of that event is compromised by the temporality of its narration as well as the temporality of its entry into Clamence's consciousness. The central event in Clamence's confession is not an event. If we follow tradition and define an event as an occurrence in time which is in principle experiencable, then the pont Royal scene is a non-event. Although there is no doubt that the cries coming from the river were experienced by Clamence, their meaning only congealed retroactively, after he hears the laugh, or perhaps even later than that, when he sees some jetsam drifting in the ocean. To the extent that *La Chute* is a confession, then it is a confession with a peculiar echo where its centre should be.

Along with its status as the admission of a truth, the traditional confession makes other, though certainly equally implicit, claims. Not only does the confession relate a truth, but its narration is truthful. It is not enough to maintain that the referent of one's confession is true, it is essential that the narration of that truth be itself truthful. In *La Chute*, the event which is as much at the heart of Clamence's memory as it is the centre of his confession, is outside the province of truth. It is neither true nor false ; it is both, therefore neither. But what of Clamence's narrative? If some of the events he describes are not events in the traditional sense, is his description not highly conventional?

Yes and no. *La Chute* is certainly readable like a traditional novel. With a few modifications, the novel can be made recognizably realistic. It is possible, for example, to imagine *La Chute* as a dialogue. Carina Gadourek, in *Les Innocents et les coupables*, argues that the force of *La Chute* lies in its status as *dialogue*:

Car à force de considérer *La Chute* comme un monologue, on est venu à oublier qu'il s'agit en réalité d'un dialogue dont les paroles de l'inconnu ont été eliminées. Celui-ci nous semble pourtant un personnage principal au même titre que Clamence. Ce dernier ne fait que relater sa chute, mais la chute à laquelle nous assistons est celle de l'Autre.[1]

And H. Allen Whartenby[2] actually attempts to supply the interlocutor's missing words. Even if the reader were to refrain from such a strategy, that is, even if the novel is read

1. *Op.cit.*,p. 175.
2. "The Interlocutor in *La Chute* : a Key to its Meaning", *PMLA*, vol. LXXXIII, no. 5, Oct. 1968, pp. 1326-33.

simply as an extended monologue, it is by no means strikingly modern in the way Blanchot's, Robbe-Grillet's or even Breton's novels are[3]. As Yves Reuter argues in *Texte/idéologie dans* La Chute *de Camus*[4], a reasonably naive reader could read *La Chute* as if it were a realistic novel : « *[...] ce texte se conforme au type générique du roman que nous avons défini, se revendique du 'littéraire', du discours humaniste [...]*». And yet, although not obsessively self-conscious in the manner of certain modern works intent on displaying their textuality, *La Chute* does not sit squarely in the category of the realistic confession. A confession should not admit of deploying a strategy. A confession normally seeks to be read as if it were the natural expression of its author. The events it narrates, the images it creates and the author it would constitute are presumed to relate to one another in a manner so natural as to preclude the need for method. Method, as Clamence notes, is the ploy of those who have no depth : « *Quand on n'a pas de caractère, il faut bien se donner une méthode.* » (1479). And, since at the time Clamence is talking about the Nazi liquidation of seventy-five thousand Jews, method is not simply a substitute for character. It is also a vehicle for the commission of a crime. Ignoring for the moment the numerous crimes peppering *La Chute*, let me note that, although all literature clearly employs various kinds of narrative strategies, traditionally the novel and specifically the confession genre, has striven to present itself as devoid of method. Method is artifice, consequently,

---

3. I must temper my statement in the light of Brian T. Fitch's enlightening article, « Une Voix qui se parle... ». One of his many interesting observations is that *structurally*, *La Chute* resembles the Nouveau Roman : « *La critique n'a pas assez insisté, à notre goût, sur ce processus de désintégration de la substance du récit, qui s'annonce, d'ailleurs, bien avant les dernières pages du roman. Le processus rapproche* La Chute, *au niveau formel de sa structure, du Nouveau Roman.* » (*Albert Camus*, n° 3, « Sur *La Chute* », 1970, pp. 70-1). My reading of *La Chute* could, in fact, be understood as an elaboration upon Fitch's sense of the modernity of the novel in its formal structure.

4. Yves REUTER, *Texte/idéologié dans* La Chute *de Camus* (Paris, Lettres Modernes, coll. « Archives des Lettres Modernes », 1980), p. 42.

when a text is engaged in seeking to establish the truth, artifice is a crime.

As opposed to the traditional confession, *La Chute* thematizes its strategy. In fact, the final two chapters are little else than an elaborate confession of the mechanism of confession. Clamence's method is to lay bare his method. He admits to his interlocutor what no interlocutor should know : that confession is a narrative and, like all narrative, it obeys internal textual canons in principle indifferent to the truth they profess to convey.

The last chapter begins with a discussion of truth. Clamence's first observation is only mildly disturbing : « *Non, je ne plaisante qu'à moitié. Je sais ce que vous pensez : il est bien difficile de démêler le vrai du faux dans ce que je raconte.* » (1535). There follows one of the many ellipses which form a strange network of silence in the book. Having divided people into three categories according to their posture towards truth, Clamence continues:

> Qu'importe, après tout? Les mensonges ne mettent-ils pas finalement sur la voie de la vérité? Et mes histoires, vraies ou fausses, ne tendent-elles pas toutes à la même fin, n'ont-elles pas le même sens? Alors, qu'importe qu'elles soient vraies ou fausses si, dans les deux cas, elles sont significatives de ce que j'ai été et de ce que je suis. On voit parfois plus clair dans celui qui ment que dans celui qui dit vrai. La vérité, comme la lumière, aveugle. Le mensonge, au contraire, est un beau crépuscule, qui met chaque objet en valeur. (1535)

What may at first appear to be a revolutionary claim for a confessor to make is, if it were to stop here, the most traditional of statements. As it stands, the above quotation merely restates the Christian version of the fall. In Christian dogma, man, having fallen from grace, must undergo the rigours of incarnation in a human form which of necessity subject him to all the drives and temptations of the flesh before he can complete the circle and re-enter Eden. Similarly, Clamence seems to be asserting that his lies are merely a detour intended to enhance the truth it ultimately serves. As in Christianity (or in Hegelian dialectics), negativity is tolerated, even welcomed, as long as it ultimately negates itself in a movement which is fundamentally phototropic. As long as truth and falsehood are in principle distinguishable, in the present or at the occasion of a future revelation which retroactively organizes the present, the relation to truth is intact. And such appears to be the thrust of Clamence's declaration. That is, until he qualifies it further : « *D'ailleurs, je n'aime plus que les confessions, et les auteurs de confession écrivent surtout pour ne pas se confesser, pour ne rien dire de ce qu'ils savent. Quand ils prétendent passer aux aveux, c'est le moment de se méfier, on va maquiller le cadavre.* » (1535-6). The form of Clamence's assertion is classic[5]. It is a paradox of the type occurring when a Roman says that all Romans lie. The form is ancient ; the effect is thoroughly modern. For when a confession claims that confessors write especially to avoid confessing, two things occur : First, the truth value of *La Chute* is rendered undecidable. Second, the status of writing in the text is called into question. As opposed to the oral confession of the various Christian churches, the literary confessions to which I have been referring are all written. Therefore, when Clamence hints at a filiation between the questionable status of truth in confessions and the fact of their having been written, he is beginning to transform *La Chute* from an Existentialist (or anti-Existentialist) tract to a monument attesting to the frustrating and seductive mobility of artifice.

Clamence claims to be a lawyer. Both in his former life and in the present of the novel, Clamence pleads cases. As I

5. J. Lévi-Valensi (*op. cit.*) is sensitive to the violence wrought by Clamence's confession. Although her analysis differs from mine, I owe much to her astute observations concerning the nature of language in *La Chute*.

Another excellent study of Camus' manipulation of the resources of language is : Roger QUILLIOT, « Albert Camus ou les difficultés du langage », *Albert Camus*, n° 2, « Langue et langage », 1969, p. 101. See also Maurice BLANCHOT, « La Confession dédaigneuse », *N.N.R.F.*, n° 48, déc. 1956, p. 1053.

noted earlier, a lawyer is an intermediary between his client and those judging him. Oblivious to the guilt or innocence of his client, a good lawyer should be able to mount a defence by the sheer power of his rhetoric. He is, of course, grateful for facts, witnesses, etc. But such evidence is merely embellishment. Like a writer, a lawyer is not judged by the raw material at his disposal, but by how he weaves that material into a text.

A trial lawyer, such as Clamence, defends (or prosecutes) criminals. His role assumes that a crime has been committed. The notion of a crime is, of course, central to *La Chute*. The biblical fall occurs because Adam and Eve defy God's prohibition. Their fall is punishment for a transgression. Similarly, Clamence's monologue argues that his fall resulted from his transgression of an ethical code when he failed to aid the woman in black. But crime in *La Chute* is not limited to this problematic scene.

Needless to say, Clamence's description of his pre-fall existence is clearly an indictment of his complicity with the criminals he defended. There is no need to summarize Clamence's Paris years. The novel is quite clear on the hypocrisy of his obsessional defence of the impoverished. Let us, however, shift our gaze from the kinds of crimes Clamence the lawyer deals with to the crimes of Clamence the narrator.

Early in the novel, after the narrator has plied his interlocutor with gin and talk, he makes a comment which most likely goes unnoticed the first time the novel is read. Discussing the bartender, Clamence says : « *Voyez, par exemple, au-dessus de sa tête, sur le mur du fond, ce rectangle vide qui marque la place d'un tableau décroché. Il y avait là, en effet, un tableau, et particulièrement intéressant, un vrai chef-d'œuvre. Eh bien, j'étais présent quand le maître de céans l'a reçu et quand il l'a cedé.* » (1476). Although the reader (or his representative, the interlocutor) has no clue to the reference of Clamence's aside, at least two observations can be made. A picture enters the text by its absence and the ape who tends bar at *Mexico-City* is somehow involved with it. *Mexico-City* is a sailors' bar in a port city. Ports are usually viewed as breeding grounds for moral turpitude. A place which is unstable, where objects have no place but are always on their way somewhere else, is also a place associated with transgression. Crimes do not befall a port, they are constitutive of its identity. A port is not the site of transgression. Inasmuch as it is not a place in the proper sense, it is the transgression of the notion of place. Like their denizens, the sailors, ports are not proper. They have no propriety since their essence is not to be the kind of stable landmark Clamence finds in the Greek archipelago but the opposite, the empty space of exchange.

So in a bar in Amsterdam, an empty space signals the absence of a painting. A painting, which is to figure in the novel at several seminal points, enters the narrative by its absence. But it is not simply absent. A mark on the wall attests to its former place in *Mexico-City*. Presumably the painting had once been present, it once had a place proper to it. Now, however, all that remains is a visible but ambiguous trace. In this city of exchange, it too changed hands. We are told that the bartender received it and eventually passed it on. The bartender, who only several pages ago, was the fatuous ape presiding over the Tower of Babel, gains in complexity. Besides grunting as he dispenses gin, he has a hand in the art trade.

The painting next enters the narrative at the end of the second chapter. Having described the haunting laugh which smacked him on the pont des Arts, Clamence appears to be lost in thought. As is often the case in the novel, an ellipsis marks the place where the narrator either loses his train of thought or appears to. Either by ruse or by weakness, Clamence, the master of language, periodically leaves an empty space in his confession to mark the spot where language failed him. These ellipses are like bridges or like hollow rectangles on a wall, signalling a hinge of absence. Having alluded to the doubleness of his smile and having tripped on some inarticulable thought, Clamence continues:

Comment? Pardonnez-moi, je pensais à autre chose. Je vous reverrai demain, sans doute. Demain, oui, c'est cela. Non, non, je ne puis rester. D'ailleurs, je suis appelé en consultation par l'ours brun que vous voyez là-bas. Un honnête homme, à coup sûr, que la police brime vilainement, et par pure perversité. Vous estimez qu'il a une tête de tueur? Soyez sûr que c'est la tête de l'emploi. Il cambriole, aussi bien, et vous serez surpris d'apprendre que cet homme des cavernes est spécialisé dans le trafic des tableaux. En Hollande, tout le monde est spécialiste en peintures et en tulipes. Celui-ci, avec ses airs modestes, est l'auteur du plus célèbre des vols de tableau. Lequel? Je vous le dirai peut-être. Ne vous étonnez pas de ma science. Bien que je sois juge-pénitent, j'ai ici un violon d'Ingres : je suis le conseiller juridique de ces braves gens.   (1493-4)

Another shady character joins the menagerie which populates *Mexico-City*. Like the ape, he appears to have no interiority. There is an uncomplicated analogy between his appearance and his actions. He engages in the traffic of stolen paintings. The puzzle posed by the first mention of a painting which once hung above the bar begins to be solved. Apparently, the bear stole the painting and the ape fenced it. The ape, consequently, is not simple. He too is an intermediary. Like the other bridges in *La Chute*, he is a conduit whereby objects are exchanged. Specifically, the object is a stolen work of art. The visible absence of the first chapter is not identified as a painting which had been taken from its rightful place by a primitive denizen of Amsterdam's less fashionable haunts. Although the thief is anonymous, his crime is famous. In fact, his theft is described as though it itself were a work of art – the bear is called the author of his theft. At this point of his monologue, Clamence is most likely assumed to be indulging his penchant for the defence of the poor and vulnerable. However, read in the context of the first scene in which the painting was mentioned, the painting, its theft, its absence and the use of the word *author* to describe the person who stole it begin to acquire a different significance. Beyond the insights if might offer concerning Clamence's propensity for the defence of the indefensible, the series of images centred around the painting is capable of constituting a framework of meaning which is independent of that illusion of psychological depth which Clamence's monologue is ceaselessly engaged in exposing.

The next time the painting surfaces its appearance is so cryptic that for all intents and purposes it goes unnoticed. Pages before Clamence avows that his love of confessors stems from their mendacity, he is describing the appearance of a new obsession. With his fall proceeding at an accelerating pace, the thought of death bursts into his life. Interestingly, it is not death itself which occupies him, but the possibility that he might die not having confessed all his lies:

Une crainte ridicule me poursuivait, en effet : on ne pouvait mourir sans avoir avoué tous ses mensonges. Non pas à Dieu, ni à un de ses représentants, j'étais au-dessus de ça, vous le pensez bien. Non, il s'agissait de l'avouer aux hommes, à un ami, ou à une femme aimée, par exemple. Autrement, et n'y eût-il qu'un seul mensonge de caché dans une vie, la mort le rendrait définitif. Personne, jamais plus, ne connaîtrait la vérité sur ce point puisque le seul qui la connût était justement le mort, endormi sur son secret.　　　　　　　　　　　　　　　　　　　　(1519)

Since the traditional concept of confession entails the revelation of a truth, Clamence's consternation is in keeping with the purported nature of his narrative. If he is indeed making a confession, not to God, but to humanity, then to die before he is finished would be to die tainted with falsehood. Confession is a kind of baptism. Unless one is thoroughly cleansed, death interrupts the process and leaves an indelible mark. It is therefore perfectly logical that the author of a confession should abhor the idea of an unrevealed lie. Of course, read with the hindsight of Clamence's assertion concerning the truth value of confessions, his fear seems contrived. And indeed, as the passage continues, it becomes clear that Clamence has just been dangling one of the many lures with which he tempts his interlocutor:

Ce meurtre absolu d'une vérité me donnait le vertige. Aujourd'hui, entre parenthèses, il me donnerait plutôt des plaisirs délicats. L'idée, par exemple, que je suis seul à connaître ce que tout le monde cherche et que j'ai chez moi un objet qui a fait courir en vain trois polices est purement délicieuse.   (1519)

Whereas previously the thought of a truth's death would have horrified Clamence, in the present of the narrative he claims it would delight him. This statement is, of course, similar to his later avowal of affection for confessors. Just as a confessor admitting that all confessors lie creates a logical whirligig, so to tell an interlocutor that the teller revels in being the only one to know something is a self-negating statement.

The object referred to is the stolen painting. Once again, only the most astute reader could be expected to make the necessary connections during a first reading. In fact, the accumulation of references to the painting, having by now attained considerable proportions, is only meaningful when, later in the book, a backward glance can effect a synthesis. Just as Clamence is not able to understand the significance of the cries bobbing down the Seine until he hears the laugh, or perhaps not until he sees a black speck on the ocean, so the reader (the interlocutor) must wait until the experience of these confessions has passed before he can lend them meaning.

It is not until the last chapter that the fragments constituting the story of the painting's theft are pieced together. It is, however, something less than a whole which emerges. Having already revealed his affection for crafty confessions, Clamence has just completed his account of his role as pope in a prisoner-of-war camp. The long paragraph which reaches the conclusion that in order to set oneself above the pope one must forgive him ends in an ellipsis. The alert reader is by now attuned to the necessity of lending an extra measure of significance to what follows Clamence's ellipses. Clamence states that whereas in the past, when he possessed considerable wealth, he invariably left his door open so as to invite the underworld to correct social and economic disequilibrium in its own way, at present, possessing nothing, he compulsively locks his door.

Having allowed the interlocutor into the closed space of his room. Clamence invites him to open a cupboard : « *À propos, voulez-vous ouvrir ce placard, s'il vous plaît. Ce tableau, oui, regardez-le. Ne le reconnaissez-vous pas? Ce sont* Les Juges intègres. » (1540).

The painting, which has popped in and out of Clamence's narrative, appears in his cupboard and gets named. Ensconced in his fortress of an apartment, the painting whose presence was announced early in the novel by its absence is paraded by Clamence like a treasure. The work with the pleonastic name is presented to the interlocutor in a gesture reminiscent of the etymology of the word truth. As Heidegger has tirelessly sought to demonstrate, the derivation of the Greek work for truth is profoundly linked to its seminal meaning : truth means un-forgetting, un-covering, revelation etc.[6]. Having brought his interlocutor so far, having seduced him into listening to a monologue whose purpose is clearly to create complicity between narrator and listener, Clamence unearths a prize. The painting, originally an outline on the wall of a bar, subsequently identified as an object of illicit exchange, is now withdrawn from a cupboard and offered as a microcosmic representation of *La Chute*. Both its presence in the narrative and the use to which Clamence puts it attest to its function as an image of the novel within the novel. Having exposed what should remain hidden,

6. Heidegger thinks that as truth was rethought by Plato, Aristotle and the Romans, it progressively lost the primal force it contained in pre-Socratic Greece. *Being and Time* is the attempt to reinstate truth within its powerful origins. For example : "*Being-true as Being-uncovering, is a way of Being for Dasein. What makes this very uncovering possible must necessarily be called 'true' in a still more primordial sense.* The most powerful phenomen of truth is first shown by the existential-ontological foundations of uncovering." (p. 263).

Clamence will proceed to engage in an extended piece of criticism. He will explain to his interlocutor the significance of this detached panel.

The painting, he explains, is part of a van Eyck altarpiece, "The Adoration of the Lamb"[7]. The panel in his cupboard « *représentait des juges à cheval venant adorer le saint animal* » (1540). It was fenced by the bartender of *Mexico-City* and for a long time « *nos juges dévots ont trôné à* Mexico-City, *au-dessus des ivrognes et des souteneurs* » (1540). At Clamence's suggestion, the ape relinquished the painting, allowing it to make its way from the Tower of Babel to Clamence's apartment. There, he explains, it enters his narrative. The judges (called just in a redundant formulation which calls into question their impartiality) are separated from their goal, the Lamb, the latter in the St. Bavon Cathedral of Ghent, the former in Clamence's cupboard. His apartment an untraversable chasm between justice and innocence, Clamence is able to revel in the correspondence between his monologue and the detached panel he is habouring.

Clamence's posture towards the painting is that of a critic. Specifically, he does not see it as a self-enclosed artifact whose purpose is to offer unmediated aesthetic pleasure. On the contrary, the painting is, for Clamence, heavily symbolic. It is something to be shown, to be exchanged and most importantly, to be analyzed. Ostensibly, his reason for finally showing the painting to the interlocutor is not simply to

7. Several interesting studies exist of the relation of *La Chute* to van Eyck's masterpiece. See, for example, Jeffrey MEYERS, "Camus' *The Fall* and van Eyck's 'The Adoration of the Lamb'", *Mosaic*, 1974, pp. 43-51 ; and, for a psychoanalytic interpretation, Jean GASSIN, « *La Chute* et le retable de 'L'Agneau mystique' : Étude de structure », *Albert Camus 80*, ed. Raymond Gay-Crosier (Gainesville, University Presses of Florida, 1980), pp. 133-39.

The real altarpiece appears to have had as ignominious a fate as its textual double. Carina Gadourek mentions in a footnote, « *Ce retable fut l'objet de honteux marchandages pendant la guerre. Il avait été confié à la France par le gouvernement belge en 1940. Le 13 septembre 1944,* Combat *annonce en première page* : 'Le célèbre retable de l'Agneau mystique a été livré aux Allemands par Abel Bonnard.' » (*op. cit.*, p. 186). See also Y. REUTER, *op. cit.*, pp. 91-3.

retroactively explain the clues he has been strewing throughout his confession, but to engage in precisely the kind of analysis I am engaging in. The painting is a symbol, it stands for something else. For one thing, it represents the gulf between innocence and justice, between the Christ child and his own guilt. However, following the narrator's lead, I think it is possible to decipher the significance of the painting a bit more.

I previously claimed that the various bridges in *La Chute* function not so much as symbols of passage from innocence to guilt, or from hypocrisy to good-faith, but as a metaphor for the metaphor. That is, a bridge, the intermediary between two points, serves the same function as that set of words whose function is to transfer meaning. A painting is, of course, essentially different from a bridge. Although both may be transformed into a symbol by a text (assuming, as I do *not*, that a word has a pre-symbolic existence), the signifier *bridge* purportedly stands for a real object, whereas "The Just Judges" represents an object whose reality is fundamentally symbolic. Like a literary text, a painting is not used as an object *per se* ; whether its use is economic, institutional, pedagogic etc., a painting, even the most abstract one, functions in relation to something else[8].

But in relation to what? Traditionally, works of art have been understood as conveyors of meaning. Art carries meaning like a woman bears a child. The meaning precedes the work of art and survives it. The work of art itself is simply the vehicle, a metaphor of sorts. If a meaning can be said to exist independently of the work of art, then it is in principle isolable from it. Therefore, in the scene under discussion, the reader (interlocutor) is left with a choice. Either "The Just Judges" means the separation of innocence and justice and is therefore isolable from that meaning, or the painting's meaning is not a parcel it bears but is insepa-

8. Let me repeat. I do not believe that it is the relation to something else which distinguishes *bridge* from *painting*. Both are, I maintain, referential through and through. I am merely emphasizing the impossibility of considering a painting in a novel as a non-symbolic entity.

rable from its textual dispersion.

La Chute argues convincingly for the second position. It enjoins the reader to approach the painting in Clamence's cupboard not as an insular image whose meaning can be derived independently of a reading of the novel, but as an image fully integrated into and articulated by a narrative which alone is capable of lending it *literary* meaning. I underline literary because I wish to emphasize that the literary meaning of an image is always a supplement to its meaning in the culture. The notion that the panel means something like "the separation of judgment from innocence" is an instance of the convergence of a possible cultural meaning with a partial textual meaning. Doubtless, a chasm between innocence and judgment is a meaning inscribed in *La Chute*, perhaps most powerfully in this image of *La Chute* within *La Chute*. To stop there, however, would be to do the novel a severe disservice. Even though I agree that "The Just Judges" is indeed a metaphor for distance, the distance in question is not *simply* the space between innocence and justice.

Let us summarize the successive manifestations of the painting. It first appears as an outline on the wall of *Mexico-City*. The vague trace it leaves introduces the painting into the text as an absence. In fact, the casual mention made of the painting makes of its absence an absence. The absence is not seen as such, that is, as the absence of "The Just Judges", until many pages later, when Clamence makes his revelation. The painting is mentioned again at the end of the second chapter. Clamence has just described the laugh he heard on the pont des Arts. He is relating a feeling of doubleness he experienced upon getting home, « *Mon image souriait dans la glace, mais il me sembla que mon sourire était double...* » (1493). The notion of doubleness is, by dint of proximity, related to one of the numerous ellipses in the novel. Although one interpretation of his double reflection would concentrate on Clamence's budding realization of his hypocrisy, I would rather focus on the surface, textual position of this image. As a subsequent scene which it is supposed to have followed by several years. I have likened this structure to Freud's *Nachträglichkeit*, in which a posterior event is actually the cause of an earlier event's consolidation as an identifiable event. Similarly, the "real" cause of Clamence's fall, his failure to lend succour to the young woman, does not appear as such in the narrative until a subsequent event established it as causal. The second event, the cause of its cause, is the laugh. The scene describing it ends with an ellipsis. Following the ellipsis, Clamence appears to be lost in thought. The reader presumes that his reverie is focused on the pont Royal scene, but there is no corroboration in the text. Clamence simply states that he was thinking of something else. Responding to his interlocutor's invitation to linger a while, Clamence declines, explaining that he has a case pending the next day. His client is the thief who first set the altarpiece panel in motion. Therefore, just as Clamence is recounting the laughter scene, and his subsequent feeling of doubleness, and immediately following a hole in the text, he introduces the bestial thief of "The Just Judges". As the reader realizes that the painting stolen by the brown bear is the same one that had hung prominently in *Mexico-City*, it becomes increasingly clear that the trajectory of the painting in the text is significant. In fact, it invites an analysis similar to the one done by Lacan of the itinerary of the letter in Poe's tale, "The Purloined Letter"[9]. At the beginning of *La Chute*, while Clamence is seeking to seduce the interlocutor, he fleetingly mentions a crime that had occurred sometime in the past. Long before the interlocutor is told about what appears to be the central crime in the narrative, another crime sets the book in motion. There is nothing mysterious about the theft of a panel of a triptych. The object itself,

9. Significantly, « Le Séminaire sur *La Lettre volée* » is the first piece in Lacan's *Écrits* (Paris, Seuil, 1966). For a critique of Lacan's reading of Poe, especially as it insists on the indivisibility of the letter and the safety of its passage, see Derrida's « Le Facteur de la vérité » in *La Carte postale* (Paris, Flammarion, 1980).

however, will not appear in the text until the last chapter. We
will then learn that it passed from the bear to the ape and
finally ended up in the hands of Clamence. The textual
sequence of the painting's manifestations is : middleman,
thief, Clamence. The place from where it is absent is a bar in
a port ; its caretaker is a fence. In this disreputable locus of
trade and exchange, a stolen painting begins its journey in
La Chute as a trace.

The brown bear is more than a thief. Or rather, his larceny
is described as a creative act : « *Celui-ci, avec ses airs
modestes, est l'auteur du plus célèbre des vols de tableau.* »
(1493-4). The thief did not simply steal the panel, he
authored its theft. The painting, a van Eyck, has two
creators : van Eyck and the bear. But in fact, as far as *La
Chute* is concerned, it has only one source. Its textual existence owes nothing to van Eyck. Clamence's description of
the bear as the author of the most famous theft of a
painting is not mere metaphor. The bear's theft brought the
painting into the novel ; and since we are in no way
concerned with a real painting, his theft is indeed a kind of
authorial creation.

The next mention of the painting is relatively cryptic. When
Clamence suggests that the horror he used to experience at
the thought that a truth might be murdered had been transformed into delight, he is, in part, referring to "The Just
Judges" : « *L'idée, par exemple, que je suis seul à connaître
ce que tout le monde cherche et que j'ai chez moi un objet
qui a fait courir en vain trois polices est purement délicieuse.* » (1519). The object in question is, of course, the
painting he has ensconced in his cupboard. Once again, it is
a reference all but the most astute of readers would miss
upon a first reading. The narrative thread joining these relatively isolated appearances of the painting and constituting
its journey through the novel is the specular opposite of the
one Ariadne used to allow Theseus to find his way out of the
labyrinth. Ariadne's thread followed Theseus to the centre of
the cave and consequently became a trace allowing Theseus

to go back over his steps. Unlike Ariadne's thread, the one joining the images constitutive of the sub-narrative of the painting does not materialize until the centre has been reached. The thread does not follow in the wake of a journey ; it appears at the journey's end.

There are two major revelation scenes in *La Chute*. The first, of course, is Clamence's confession of his cowardice. The second is the literal and figurative revelation of "The Just Judges". It is in the last chapter that the various clues concerning the identity of the painting stolen by the bear and fenced by the ape are pieced together. The sequence of scenes constitutive of the sub-plot woven around the panel appear, at first glance, to be analogous to that of the classic detective novel[10]. As in detective fiction, there is a mystery of sorts. Clues are scattered throughout the novel until, during the scene in Clamence's apartment, the web is untangled and the truth apparently revealed. In fact, the opposite occurs. Although the sub-plot concerning "The Just Judges" does indeed resemble a classic mystery, the resemblance is parodic. The painting sub-plot mimics a mystery plot in order to undermine the fundamental presupposition of mystery. Certainly in detective fiction, and arguably in fiction in general, mystery is structured by its imminent negation. Mystery is a propaedeutic to revelation. Many kinds of plot, and most vividly detective plots, create mystery as a narrative strategy totally dominated by its telos : the illumination of what was previously obscure. This is precisely the dynamic structure of truth as described by Heidegger[11]. Truth is revelation, illumination, epiphany etc. All these metaphors for truth, and many others, inscribe the notion of truth within the metaphorics of light[12]. When

10. The detective genre has been the object of serious theoretical work of late. A good starting-point would be *Littérature*, n° 49, « Le Roman policier », févr. 1983.

11. Besides the previous reference to *Being and Time*, another good source for Heidegger's definition of truth as un-concealment, especially as it relates to art, is "The Origin of the Work of Art" in *Poetry, Language, Thought* (New York, Harper and Row, 1971).

12. For the convoluted relation between metaphor and light, see « Les

something is revealed to be true, when one exits Plato's cave and stands in the sun, obscurity and its concomitant, the possibility of illusion, are burned away by the penetrating light. Earlier in the novel, Clamence describes a similar relation to light when he reminisces about Greece:

Vous vous trompez, cher, le bateau file à bonne allure. Mais le Zuydersee est une mer morte, ou presque. Avec ses bords plats, perdus dans la brume, on ne sait où elle commence, où elle finit. Alors, nous marchons sans aucun repère, nous ne pouvons évaluer notre vitesse. Nous avançons, et rien ne change. Ce n'est pas de la navigation, mais du rêve.
Dans l'archipel grec, j'avais l'impression contraire. Sans cesse, de nouvelles îles apparaissaient sur le cercle de l'horizon. Leur échine sans arbres traçait la limite du ciel, leur rivage rocheux tranchait nettement sur la mer. Aucune confusion ; dans la lumie # \re précise, tout était repère.   (1523)

As opposed to the murky northern sea, the Mediterranean is clearly defined. The clarity of the sun and the sea render illusion impossible. There are landmarks in Greece ; whereas on the Zuider Zee it is impossible to gauge one's speed because there are no reliable standards against which to measure it. In Greece light not only illuminates it also constitutes a standard. Illusion is only possible when there is no truth to serve as exemplar. In Greece there is no confusion because truth rains down from the sky[13].

Fleurs de la rhétorique : L'Héliotrope » in « La Mythologie blanche ». For example, « *Métaphore veut donc dire héliotrope, à la fois mouvement tourné vers le soleil et mouvement tournant du soleil.* » (p. 299).
13. An interesting study of Camus' relation to the Mediterranean Sea and to Greece is François Bousquet's *Camus le méditerranéan Camus l'ancien* (Sherbrooke, Québec, Éditions Naaman, 1977). Bousquet's book begins with a 1933 poem by Camus, « Poème sur la Méditerranée ». The poem ends as follows:

Pressante Antiquité
Méditerranée, ah! mer Méditerranée
Seuls, nus, sans secrets, tes fils attendent la mort,
La mort te les rendra, purs, enfin.

But the novel is set in Amsterdam. When, in this ambiguous Dutch landscape Clamence offers to reveal the little
truth he has been hiding all along, his gesture is wrought
with ambiguity. The painting, ostensibly a symbol of the
distance between innocence and judgment, is removed from
Clamence's cupboard. Although the bear had been previously described as the author of the panel's theft, the interlocutor is now informed that it is in fact a van Eyck, part of
"The Adoration of the Lamb". Clamence proceeds to interpret the significance of the painting. Much of what he says
is straightforward and has already been discussed. Not
wishing to disparage the importance of the painting as a
metaphor for Clamence's career as judge-penitent, I will
nevertheless focus on another part of his description.

The painting, he asserts, was replaced by an excellent
copy because the original was never found. Those who file
by "The Adoration of the Lamb" view a simulacrum. They do
not, however, know that they are seeing a copy « *parce que
parmi ceux qui défilent devant* l'Agneau Mystique, *personne
ne saurait distinguer la copie de l'original [...]*» (1540).
Clamence draws the obvious conclusion : « *[...] de cette
manière, je domine. De faux juges sont proposés à l'admira-
tion du monde et je suis seul à connaître les vrais.* » (1540).
His conclusion would be correct were he in Greece. But in
Holland things aren't that simple.

Clamence claims that the painting has been replaced by a
copy. This copy, which is occupying the space in the St.
Bavon Cathedral formerly occupied by the original, is so
good that no one can distinguish it from the van Eyck. No
one, including the interlocutor, is able to distinguish original
from imitation. We have reached a crucial point in the novel
whose importance will be missed if the narrative is read as if
it were a realistic novel. Such a reader would object to the
suggestion that copy and original are indistinguishable. It is

---

Another worthwhile analysis of Camus' relation to Greece, especially
of the similarities between *La Chute* and ancient tragedy, is John J.
Lakich's, "Tragedy and Satanism in Camus' *La Chute*", *Symposium*,
vol. XXIV, no. 3, "Albert Camus II", Fall 1970, pp. 262-76.

perhaps true that experts are usually able to identify an original (although, and this is decisive, their accuracy is not total) ; art detectives are, however, irrelevant here. *La Chute* does not claim fidelity to the world. If anything, the novel is constantly alerting the reader to its counter-intuitive functioning. If we use the term rigorously, as Derrida uses it, the *text* of *La Chute* is precisely that part of the novel which does not allow itself to be subsumed by the naturalistic presuppositions which have guided the interpretation of literature until recently. Consequently, when Clamence says that "The Just Judges" was replaced by a facsimile indistinguishable from the original, it is not to the world that we must turn for a means of interpreting that statement. Instead, we must seek to elucidate its meaning and its force within the microcontext of the book.

Two things are of immediate interest : one, that the truth brought to light by Clamence concerns the relation of original to copy ; two, that Clamence earlier referred to the thief of the painting as the author of its crime. Authorship and crime are somehow brought together within a structure of revelation. The author of a crime is one who has allowed Clamence to acquire, via the intermediary of the bartender, a work of art which is indistinguishable from the copy which hangs in a cathedral. From the St. Bavon Cathedral, to *Mexico-City,* and finally to Clamence's cupboard, the journey of the painting appears to be decidedly downhill. That is, until we remember Clamence's confession concerning confessions. Confessors lie, he states. If we provisionally suspend judgment of this logical *mise en abîme* and simply take Clamence at his word, then, at the very least, it is clear that his word is not trustworthy. At any given moment he may be lying ; or, of course, he may not. Consequently, when he says that the painting in his cupboard is the original and a perfect copy is displayed in the cathedral, there is cause to be sceptical.

If the copy and the original are indistinguishable, then it is conceivable that Clamence is actually holding the copy. I am not claiming that he is, I am simply arguing that the novel makes the choice between original and copy impossible. Given Clamence's proclivity towards mendacity, and given the (possible) existence of a perfect copy, there is no way for the interlocutor, or the reader, to accurately gauge the authenticity of the painting lodged in the cupboard. The truth which Clamence claims to keep hidden, but which, in fact, he displays continually, is purely un-Hellenic. It bears no relation to those islands whose spine is a clear and sure landmark. There is no perspective, no vantage point, in the novel from which to determine the genuineness of the panel. It is neither an original, nor is it a copy ; it is the unavailability of a scale with which to measure the distance between a thing and its imitation.

What, then, does Clamence keep ensconced in his cupboard? The question "What?" is one of the seminal questions of philosophy[14]. It is always asked within the horizon of a possible revelation. To ask "What?" is to assume that the question is answerable ontologically, with an answer respectful of the identity of the object. And since the question "What?" always refers to a potential answer concerning the being of an object, the question also refers to the origin of the object. As Heidegger and Derrida have both argued, the question of being is always the question of origin. The being of an object is the history of its genesis. The point of origin, the "Where?" whence an object came, is constitutive of its "What?". In fact, the question "What?" contains within itself the other two seminal questions of philosophy, "Where?" and "When?". A thing has an origin which is both a place and a moment in time. The being of an object is the combination of the mode of its presentation, its source, and the temporality of its constitution[15]. To ask, therefore, "What,

14. In *Being and Time*, Heidegger says, "Existentalia *and categories are the two basic possibilities for characters of Being. The entities which correspond to them require different kinds of primary interrogation respectively ; any entity is either a 'who' (existence) or a 'what' (presence-at-hand in the broadest sense).*" (p. 71).

15. Temporality and Ontology are two faces of the notion of *pres-*

then, does Clamence keep ensconced in his cupboard?" is to assume that the question is answerable within the horizon of a certain definition of being.

A painting's relation to its creator appears to be a simple version of the far more complex relation of a thing in general to its origin. After all, a painting did not exist before it was painted, and once painted, and signed, there is no doubt as to its creator. The seminal questions "What?" and "Where?" are, it would appear, answerable unambiguously when the object in question is a painting. In fact, painting, or art in general, seems to be an instance of the identity of "What?" and "When?", since, as the term implies, a creator is both a giver of identity (makes the painting itself, hence creates its "whatness") and the agent of its coming into being (creates the temporal span of a before and after, hence situates the painting in a temporal sequence).

The painting in Clamence's cupboard does not, however, allow itself to be encompassed by the temporal and ontological horizon implied by the notion of creation. Since it is in principle impossible to determine whether it is an original or a copy, there are no standards by which to judge its relation to its creator. Clamence's casual reference to the thief as an "author" is perhaps less frivolous than it might appear at first. For although van Eyck is indeed the creator of "The Just Judges", the essential ambiguity established by a combination of a perfect copy and a narrator who is untrustworthy makes of the bear the author of the painting in Clamence's cupboard. The textual network of indecidability which generates and is generated by the image of a lost painting is indeed a crime. The bear's theft is not so much of a painting but of the means to establish its identity. Van Eyck did not create the painting in the cupboard; as far as *La Chute* is concerned, *the possible theft of the painting is its origin*. In fact, the possibility of even thinking of van Eyck as its

ence. Presence is the proximity and propriety of Being as well as the integrity of its deployment in the indivisibility of the present. The presence of the present is Derrida's central reservation concerning Heidegger's work. See « Les Fins de l'Homme » in *Marges*.

creator is subsequent to the painting's trajectory through *La Chute*. It is only after it enters the novel as a void, after it passes through several obscure references, and then emerges as a truth in danger of extinction that "The Just Judges" is identified. Its identity does not precede the network of its textual manifestation but is a result of it. "The Just Judges" is not stolen first and then replaced by a perfect copy ; its replacement creates the possibility of its identification. Just as Clamence's fall occurs after what succeeds it, the constitution of the panel is posterior to its theft.

"The Just Judges" and Clamence's fall are both structured by a counter-intuitive temporality. Both do not appear as such in the novel but, on the contrary, become their tenuous selves after lengthy textual elaboration. Furthermore, the relation between painting and copy is analogous to that between the pont Royal scene and the pont des Arts scene. In both cases, a subsequent event (the laughter in one case, the copy in the other) is both constitutive of the original event and indistinguishable from it. Just as the painting's theft is, in Clamence's words, « *ce meurtre absolu d'une vérité* » (1519), so the deployment of the two bridge scenes makes it impossible to determine the truth of the origin of Clamence's fall. Clamence falls after he has fallen, or falls before he has fallen. The precise temporality is not important. What matters is that the concept of *a first time* (When?), so essential to the constitution of identity (What?), is distended beyond recognition.

THE THIRD QUESTION

WHY? That is, after all, the third seminal question of philosophy. Why did Camus write *La Chute*? This question is, of course, unanswerable. Although I submit that all novels do so, it is clear that *La Chute* thematizes the absence of its author. The question, however, will not go away with such a deft stroke. Even if the issue of the author's intentions is unresolvable, the question remains.

"Why?" concerns a fundamental critical problem on two levels. At the same time that the question of an author's intentions obstinately refuses to disappear, the question of the critic's intentions becomes pressing. Since it is becoming increasingly difficult to claim that literature conveys messages, and since the practice of Deconstruction has even tampered with the heretofore unassailable unity and identity of a literary text, is the critic's role merely to be negative? That is, is the critic who espouses many of the recent critical and philosophical positions loosely gathered under the name of Post-Structuralism condemned to demonstrate how novels don't mean, how they don't hold together, how they are not even equivalent to themselves.

Yes and no. Yes because the direction of twentieth century continental thought is certainly towards a radical questioning of those unities which have been traditionally assumed to be natural hence essentially unavailable for interrogation. It is simply impossible, for many of us, to continue to conceptualize literature as a pregnant woman, heavy with preformed meaning. No because if taken to an extreme, the Deconstruction attitude risks becoming facile and monolithic. It is not enough in a novel such as *La Chute*, for example, to indicate those points in the text wherein a certain image or set of images become a metaphor for

Derrida's *writing*.

It is precisely because the opposite of meaning is meaninglessness that I am not interested in any effort to disrupt meaning. Deconstruction is not nihilistic, its goal is not simply to seep into meaning and warp it internally. Derrida repeatedly signals the *productive* resources of Deconstruction. For example, in *Positions* he says: « *La dissémination, au contraire, pour produire un nombre non-fini d'effets sémantiques, ne se laisse reconduire ni à un présent d'origine simple [...] ni à une présence eschatologique. Elle marque une multiplicité irréductible et générative.* »[1]. Specifically, if literature doesn't mean, then it does nothing at all. To deconstruct a literary text is not to deprive it of meaning. If anything, Deconstruction, in its most powerful manifestations, is actually a critical perspective allowing the *production* of a surplus of meaning. As opposed to certain traditional interpretive practices, a deconstructive approach, such as that espoused in this analysis, is especially sensitive to the way in which meaning proliferates in a literary text.

But what about "Why?"? Have I, by shifting my focus from the author to the critic, sought to finesse the issue? Deconstruction is, I think, the site for the transformation of "Why?" into "How?". By indefatigably interrogating the metaphysics of volition, Derrida has sought to generalize the notion of a text. That is, when Derrida claims that there is nothing outside the text, he is not militating for a new literary closure. He is not arguing that the critic need not concern himself with anything outside the text, but that the "outside" is itself articulated like a text. Ultimately, the most hermetic bastion of a-textuality, the will (ego, self, transcendental ego etc.) is, according to Derrida, a text to be studied. Just as "What?" implies a certain horizon of being and "When?" a certain notion of temporality, so "Why?" suggests a precise metaphysics of volition. We ask "Why?" when it is possible to ascertain motives. And even when motives are not those of a person, even when they are the functioning of natural

1. J. DERRIDA, *Positions* (Paris, Éditions de Minuit, 1972), p. 62.

law, the question "Why?" nevertheless always asks about the reason for something. To say "Why?" implies that a connection can be established between agent and product, or between law and consequence. To the extent, therefore, that there is a contestation of the very notion of agency, the "Why?" becomes relativized. I may not be able to discover why an author (including the one writing now) wrote in a certain way, but I can, more or less, attempt to understand how a text works (and doesn't work). If I can do so, even minimally, I will have answered the question "Why?" as well as I can. In a novel, given the inability, or the refusal, to ponder authorial intentions, *"Why?" gets displaced onto the text* and becomes "How?".

La Chute thematizes the absence of the author. It therefore denatures the question "Why?". Rather than speculate about "Why?" *La Chute* is the way it is, or what amounts to the same thing, to wonder about Clamence's motivations, I think the text enjoins the reader to seek to establish connections within the text. Consequently, having noticed a structural similarity between two central images in the novel, the stolen painting and the bridge scenes, it is necessary to see how they fit into the fabric of the novel. The questions one is tempted to ask : "Why does Camus invert the order of the two bridge scenes, and Why does he render the origin and ontological status of 'The Just Judges' undecidable?" become : "How do these images function in the novel?".

Let us return to the beginning of *La Chute*. It will be recalled that this analysis began with a discussion of the textual (in the large sense) implications of the various images constituting the first chapter. I emphasized the importance of the novel's setting (Amsterdam and *Mexico-City*), of the bartender, and of the narrator's interest in language. Although it is not until the beginning of the second chapter that the narrator describes himself as a lawyer, it is clear from the beginning (« *À moins que vous ne m'autorisiez à plaider votre cause [...]* » [1475]) that he practises the profession of law. A lawyer bears a structural similarity to a port because both are sites of exchange. We have seen that *Mexico-City*, besides being a watering-spot for sailors, is also a location where stolen works of art (or their copies) are fenced. The textual Amsterdam, then, as opposed to the real Dutch city, is a place facilitating the intersection of crime, language, and exchange. It is here that Clamence accosts his silent interlocutor and seduces him. It is here that he practises his profession, where like a twentieth century Satan, he lures others into an underworld whose fabric is a highly mobile marketplace for a troupe of signs.

Clamence is repeatedly called upon to translate. Whether he translates from Dutch into French, from the inarticulate grunts of the bartender into language, from the vernacular into the legal code, or from the silence of the bridge into the discourse of innocence and guilt via the intermediary of the laugh, Clamence's function in his own confession is to facilitate the passage from one code to another.

Clamence is aware of the centrality of language in his narrative. To my knowledge, the best analysis of Clamence's relation to language is Jacqueline Lévi-Valensi's « *La Chute, ou la parole en procès* »[2]. Although I could not possibly summarize her meticulous argument, I would like to quote her marvellous conclusion:

Il feint, se réfugiant obstinément dans une parole dont il sait bien qu'elle est sans valeur aucune, d'y masquer son néant. Clamence n'est-il pas, en fin de compte, une allégorie de la parole : non seulement un homme qui parle, mais le langage lui-même, se livrant à la tentative désespérée de prendre possession d'un monde qu'il sait pourtant privé de sa grandeur et de son innocence? Ce qui nous renvoie sans doute à la conscience anxieuse de l'écrivain, mais affirme, paradoxalement, la valeur de l'œuvre qui, par l'éclat de cette « *parole vaine* », poursuit, en nous, son incessante interrogation.[3]

2. Art. cit.
3. *Ibid.*, pp. 54-5.

Consequently, if Clamence is not simply a figure who speaks but an allegory of language, our attention should focus on the kind of language he speaks/is.

Let us begin by observing that Clamence is not simply talkative, he is talkative in a certain way : « *J'avoue ma faiblesse pour ce mode* [l'imparfait du subjonctif], *et pour le beau langage, en général.* » (1476). Clamence has a penchant for fine speech. That is, language for him is not merely a means for communication ; it is, in addition, an adornment to meaning, a supplement to sense which he cultivates. If we are to take him at his word, always a risk in *La Chute*, Clamence uses language esthetically. He enjoys the superfluities and baroque twists of language for their own sake ; as opposed to the bartender whose limited powers of speech are practical at best, Clamence is a linguistic hobbyist. His fascination with language traces an unlikely circle. Although different from his ancestors in the Tower of Babel, who discovered that communication is not transparent, Clamence, with his overdeveloped sensitivity to language, is nevertheless aware of the risks of misunderstanding and dissimulation.

Faiblesse que je me reproche, croyez-le. Je sais bien que le goût du linge fin ne suppose pas forcément qu'on ait les pieds sales. N'empêche. Le style, comme la popeline, dissimule trop souvent de l'eczéma. Je m'en console en me disant qu'après tout, ceux qui bafouillent, non plus, ne sont pas purs. Mais oui, reprenons du genièvre.   (1476)

Clamence uses the metaphorics of depth to describe his penchant for fine speech. Style, which is to say non-teleological language, is likened to silk. Like silk, it is wont to cover an unappealing interior. Furthermore, in Clamence's simile, it is not a repulsive thing which silk hides, but a repulsive covering. Silk hides eczema, which itself (presumably) hides skin. Skin, however, is not mentioned.

Language, therefore, when removed from the register of communication, risks concealing a nauseating depth. And since there is no better way of advertising the presence of a thing than by pointing to its concealment, a certain kind of language also announces the ugliness it hides.

As such, Clamence's analysis of his own language is not noteworthy. In fact, it is simply a restatement of popular wisdom. It is not until a few pages later that Clamence's comparison becomes interesting. Having offered to accompany his silent companion home, Clamence describes his neighbourhood:

Après vous, je vous en prie. Moi, j'habite le quartier juif, ou ce qui s'appelait ainsi jusqu'au moment où nos frères hitlériens y ont fait de la place. Quel lessivage! Soixante-quinze mille juifs déportés ou assassinés, c'est le nettoyage par le vide. J'admire cette application, cette méthodique patience! Quand on n'a pas de caractère, il faut bien se donner une méthode. Ici, elle a fait merveille, sans contredit, et j'habite sur les lieux d'un des plus grands crimes de l'histoire.   (1479)

Besides defending criminals and sometimes habouring their plunder, Clamence lives on the site of the Dutch holocaust. His posture towards the Nazis' atrocities, if it is taken literally, is barbarous : he claims to admire Hitler's troops for their efficiency. Of course, if one were intent upon treating Clamence like a real human being and therefore seeking to consolidate his various textual manifestations into one coherent personality, it would be possible to read his statement in a variety of ways consistent with the profession of judge-penitent. That, however, is not my goal. Rather than impose personality where there is none, I would rather see the novel as a statement on personality. That, in fact, is the point of Clamence's comment. Method is a substitute for personality. What Clamence finds admirable in the Nazis is that lacking character, they found a serviceable replacement. Regardless of the meaning accruing to the word *character*, it is always one suggesting depth. Character is what lies beneath a sometimes illusory surface. And even when one's exterior is not misleading, the relation of exterior to interior is always hierarchical. An exterior is accurate insofar as it corresponds to an interior, not vice versa. In other words, truth is depth, surface the possibility of error. Method, in Clamence's description of the Nazis, takes the place of an absent interior. It is because there is nothing deep inside that one needs to concoct strategy.

Clamence admires in the Nazis what he tongue in cheek dislikes in himself. When he chides himself for an overly developed sense of linguistic style, when he likens fine speech to silk hiding eczema, he employs the same metaphoric system he deploys in describing the Dutch holocaust. In both cases, a highly organized, perhaps attractive, surface hides a repulsive interior. Furthermore, in both cases, that which is hidden is absent. Just as silk does not hide a thing but a disgusting subsurface surface, so the Nazis' method conceals a lack of character. We may conclude that in the series of metaphors Clamence is developping, structure is the surface equivalent of an absent depth. Or, stated otherwise, surface is the structural component of absence. Absence *is* surface inasmuch as it is already a substitute for itself.

Clamence uses a spatial or topographical model to describe his language. My analysis of the bridge scenes and the sub-plot of the stolen painting relied on a temporal model. Both the spatial and the temporal sequences are structured by analogous, though not identical, inversions. In the painting and bridge scenes the notion of origin is problematized ; a temporality is suggested in which an origin, or a first moment in general, is in fact subsequent to its consequences. In the language references, surface, which is logically opposed to its dialectical opposite, depth, appears to be a sign pointing to a void.

I propose to attempt the articulation of the temporal and topological inversions not only with each other, but with the overall form of the novel. Let us begin cautiously. A page or so after the previous quotation, Clamence and his friend are walking in the rain. It has been raining for days. Like the night when he failed to come to the aid of the woman on the pont Royal, the normal ambiguity of an urban evening is highlighted by rain. Like many a murky gloaming in *La Chute*, this evening is devoid of perspective. Except, perhaps, for that offered by the drink which is continually imbibed in the novel : « *Heureusement, il y a le genièvre, la seule lueur dans ces ténèbres. Sentez-vous la lumière dorée, cuivrée, qu'il met en vous? J'aime marcher à travers la ville, le soir, dans la chaleur du genièvre.* » (1479-80). At the beginning of the novel, gin first affords Clamence access to the interlocutor. From that initial mention, gin is constantly in *La Chute*. In a narrative so concerned with water, it is interesting that gin is the only alcoholic drink mentioned. Gin's salient feature is its transparency. Although it is highly alcoholic, it has an innocuous appearance. In fact, gin looks like water. Needless to say, *La Chute*'s use of water is at variance with the biblical tradition on which it is a commentary. As opposed to his namesake, Jean-Baptiste Clamence does not use water to cleanse the soul, but to sully it. Rivers, canals, the Zuider Zee, rain etc., are all suggestive of the dangers of indeterminacy. Even the Nazis' crime is described as a cleansing : « *Quel lessivage!* » (1479). Water, which traditionally cleans the surface as it symbolically cleanses the soul, is used in *La Chute* to refract light so that clear vision is impossible. Gin, which looks like water, is taken internally and also affects vision. The woman who presumably drowned (I am cautious about her death. We never see her drown. The issue, however, is not pressing. Whether she died is unimportant. Clamence is only concerned with his reaction to her leap.) died by ingesting an excessive amount of what, in moderate doses, is essential to life. While the water swallowed by the girl killed her, drinking gin offers a subtle illumination. Gin is not light ; gin is a glimmer of light. It is a pale illumination, but the only one available in rain-soaked Amsterdam. In a city, then, which is fundamentally turbid, a simulacrum of that which cleanses, kills, and fosters life is the only source of light. Clear gin, which can reach the brain and dull its perceptions, is also that which affords a limited, distorted, and undependable illumination. Like the painting in Clamence's cupboard, gin both mimics the trajectory of truth and removes it from the register of possible revelation. This is a perverse and telling paradox. It is perhaps the greatest accomplishment of *La Chute*, and a sign of Camus' genius which has been neglected. The Camus we confront here is far removed from the Camus of *Le Mythe de Sisyphe*. It is important to underline the difference between Clamence and the falled titan : Sisyphus is usually interpreted as representing the eternal struggle between lucidity and obscurity. Fighting the great darkness with his stone, Sisyphus is a figure for the clash between man's romantic desire for vision and the world's obstinate refusal to show itself. Gin, in *La Chute*, creates a deceptively similar, yet decisively different struggle. In the traditional reading of Camus' Sisyphus, man's confrontation with the world can be summarized as the opposition between presence and withdrawal. Specifically, in a structure akin to that described by Heidegger in "The Origin of the Work of Art", the world retracts into itself in direct proportion to man's epistemological thrusts[4]. I am suggesting a radically different deployment of illumination and obscurity. I am suggesting that « *la seule lueur* » or « *la lumière dorée, cuivrée* » offered by gin is not a muted version of the sun's light, nor is it a compromise between light and darkness. That is, it is not a Hegelian, dialectical, resolution of antithetical states. On the contrary, the illumination

---

4. Heidegger defines *earth* as self-closing and self-concealing, *world* as un-concealing or opening. The struggle between world and earth is implicit in the etymology of the Greek word for truth, ἀλήθεια. For Heidegger, it is art which relates world to earth : "*That into which the work sets itself back and which it causes to come forth in this setting back of itself we called the earth. Earth is that which comes forth and shelters. Earth, self-dependent, is effortless and untiring. Upon the earth and in it, historical man grounds his dwelling in the world. In setting up a world, the work sets forth the earth. This setting forth must be thought here in the strict sense of the word. The work moves the earth itself into the Open of a world and keeps it there. The work lets the earth be an earth.*" (*Poetry, Language, Thought*, p. 46).

afforded by gin is artificial through and through. Like the proverbial glow provided by alcohol, the copper light gin kindles is not a copy of the sun's muscular rays. In fact, in a movement analogous to the spatial and temporal logic of the bridge and painting scenes, gin casts a reserved and dappled light which creates the possibility of the classic philosophical binary opposition between vision and cecity.

The previous passage quoted continues:

Je marche des nuits durant, je rêve, ou je me parle interminablement. Comme ce soir, oui, et je crains de vous étourdir un peu, merci, vous êtes courtois. Mais c'est le trop-plein : dès que j'ouvre la bouche, les phrases coulent. Ce pays m'inspire, d'ailleurs. J'aime ce peuple, grouillant sur les trottoirs, coincé dans un petit espace de maisons et d'eaux, cerné par des brumes, des terres froides, et la mer fumante comme une lessive. Je l'aime, car il est double. Il est ici et il est ailleurs.   (1480)

Clamence habitually takes long, pointless walks. As he walks he dreams or talks to himself. Apparently, he is at times unable to distinguish between the two. This evening his endless discourse is directed to the interlocutor. Clamence apologizes for his longwindedness, fearing that it might make his companion's head swim. That is, he suspects that his monologue might have the same effect as gin. His language, previously qualified as precious, is here described as intoxicating. Furthermore, Clamence uses a telling metaphor to describe his prolixity. His sentences flow ; in fact, they are an overflow. A certain kind of language, which Clamence has likened to an enticing surface hiding/revealing absence, is now said to flow. Since Clamence has just finished extolling gin, his choice of metaphor to describe his language suggests a filiation between gin and language. Both are a kind of light, albeit a decadent and ambiguous one. They are neither a source nor a reflection, neither Plato's cave nor the sun. And yet one can read by them.

What is a judge-penitent? There are many ways to approach that question. Indeed, the asking of the question, as well as the timing of its asking, are both answers of a sort. I have refrained from posing the problem of Clamence's profession until now because to have asked the question at the beginning of my study would have been to make an assumption about La Chute which I am wary of : that it is an Existentialist novel dealing with the problem of universal guilt. Although the novel is certainly concerned with the notion of guilt, to have begun my analysis with an investigation into the meaning of judge-penitence would have risked inscribing my reading within the horizon of received interpretations. I wished to avoid analyses of the type done by Brian Masters who, approaching the question of the status of language in La Chute with a dogged refusal to see anything in the novel but a restatement of what he assumes Camus *always means*, claims that:

La Chute offers us a picture of the ultimate degradation of language employed to enslave and reduce the listener. For Camus, communication between men was the means by which they recognized each other and asserted their solidarity in the fight against an unjust world, and he could not bring himself to forgive men who use words to diminish or distort the human experience.[5]

Rather than approaching La Chute armed with presuppositions about what the novel must mean, I sought to *limit* (not exclude) certain common preconceptions, thereby allowing the novel to present itself in its surprising complexity.

Regardless of Clamence's themes, the salient feature of his confession is its wordiness. If we were to take the paradox of a confessor asserting that all confessors lie literally, it would be impossible, in principle, to say anything at all about the content of La Chute. Since nothing Clamence says could be believed *per se*, the novel would have no content. Although for reasons to be explained shortly, I am not prepared to lapse into silence on the subject of La Chute,

5. *Op. cit.*, p. 126.

were a reader to treat it like Descartes treated the world, then the text's Cogito would be, simply, itself[6].

Radicalizing his doubt, Descartes concludes that he can only trust doubt. Similarly, the confessor's paradox would preclude certainty on the reader's part concerning any aspect of *La Chute* save its phenomenal surface. Since we cannot have any confidence in *what* Clamence says, we are left to ponder the saying of what he says, or stated otherwise, his monologue. As Reuter argues in his *Texte/idéologie dans* La Chute *de Camus*, once the reader of *La Chute* is deprived of the possibility of a truth lurking behind the text, he is forced to shift his focus from the realm of meaning to the text itself : « *Le texte n'est plus support/voile d'un sens, mais produit le sens, la fiction. Sa réalité n'est pas tributaire des lois extérieures de notre monde.* »[7]. Of the text of *La Chute* there can be no doubt. And, whatever posture one may assume towards Clamence's message, whatever temporary or provisional landmark one may choose to adopt in the murk of his monologue, the only sure signpost, the only hint of Greece in Clamence's Amsterdam, is Clamence's style. His words, overflowing like the ocean would if Amsterdam's dikes were to crack, his precious, narcissistic, sententious and ultimately undecipherable style is all that remains after *La Chute* lays waste to itself. What is a judge-penitent? Beyond any question of guilt or innocence, a judge-penitent is one who talks. In a passage quoted previously, Clamence explains why the death of a truth, formerly a vertiginous thought, would now delight him. Foreshadowing his later revelation of an essentially problematic truth, Clamence says : « *L'idée, par exemple, que je suis seul à connaître ce que tout le monde cherche et que j'ai chez moi un objet qui a fait courir en vain trois polices est purement délicieuse. Mais laissons cela. À l'époque, je n'avais pas trouvé la recette et je me tourmentais.* » (1519). The recipe,

6. Derrida reads Cartesian doubt as a hyperbolic passage to the limit which, paradoxically, inscribes it in the realm of insanity. See « Cogito et histoire de la folie » in *L'Écriture et la différence* (Paris, Seuil, 1967).

7. *Op. cit.*, p. 48.

of course, is the role of judge-penitent. But, not necessarily the simple role of one who accuses himself so that he might reign over those who are equally guilty but less lucid. If that were the case, *La Chute* would be no different from the traditional confession. It is not enough to confess. As Clamence puts it, one needs a recipe. Clamence doesn't simply confess, he weaves a monologue as a chef would create a dish. The recipe Clamence says he hadn't found is not self-denigration. Or, at least, not solely that. Clamence's recipe is the fact of using a recipe. It is his style.

A few pages later, at the end of the chapter, Clamence explains : « *Voyez-vous, il ne suffit pas de s'accuser pour s'innocenter, ou sinon je serais un pur agneau. Il faut s'accuser d'une certaine manière, qu'il m'a fallu beaucoup de temps pour mettre au point [...]*» (1522). Clamence's discovery is that he is no better than the Nazis. Both indulged and perhaps revelled in a crime – the Nazis in the holocaust, Clamence in the liquidation of truth. And both substitute a kind of surface for an absent interior – the Nazis compensate for their lack of character with method, Clamence compensates for a lack of content with style. Style is method. Both are overflow. They do not mask a pre-existing crime, they *are* the commission of crime. If crime in general is the transgression of law, then crime could only reinforce the code it would disrupt. Clamence's crime is not of this kind. His crime is the transgression of the structure of transgression. As Brian T. Fitch argues in his remarkable recent book on Camus, *The Narcissistic Text*[8], "*The reader's expectations have not been merely frustrated : they have proved to have been completely unfounded. Every certainty he had thought to have acquired during the course of his reading has collapsed.*" Clamence's monologue so disfigures the confessional form that no standards are left whereby to gauge the nature and extent of the transgression. A judge-

8. Brian T. FITCH, *The Narcissistic Text. A Reading of Camus' Fiction* (Toronto, University of Toronto Press, coll. "Romance Series", 1982), pp. 83-4.

penitent is not a latter-day John the Baptist. If he were,
Clamence says, he would be as innocent as a lamb ; that is,
he would be as guilty as Christ. The difference between
Clamence and John the Baptist is subtle. It is, however,
within that subtlety that *La Chute*'s distance from a theological (or, what amounts to the same thing, an anti-
theological) text is maintained. The key word in the above
quotation, perhaps the seminal word in the entire novel, is
certain.

Clamence uses *certain* to qualify the way in which one
must accuse oneself. Rather than connoting certainty,
« *d'une certaine manière* » implies limitation. To tell a story in
a certain way is ultimately, just to tell a story. The certain
way in which a story is told is the fact of style, the idiosyncratic and artificial manipulation of language, which is the
benchmark of literature in general. Clamence assumes the
form of a traditional confession, a form promising a definite,
fixed, and determined truth, in order to effect a revelation
which is essentially cryptic. It is important to note that the
notion of style developed by *La Chute* does not involve a
dual dialectic relation between truth and absence. Such an
opposition would simply reinstate that ancient complicity
between innocence and guilt which Clamence so deftly
unravels. To accuse oneself in a certain way, to be at once
definite and not specified, is to develop a strategy which
knows nothing outside its own machinations. The closed
system of *La Chute* is the absence of a meaningful referential exterior : it is a refracted confession which denies the
reader access to that phantasmagoric, textually constituted
exterior whereby he habitually gauges his position. Since
there is no exterior within the novel, neither is there an
interior. The spatial metaphor is rendered hollow. The
remaining space is that spartan strand we call it literature.

CONCLUSION

THE Principle of Identity[1] is the text of a lecture given by Heidegger to mark the 500th anniversary of the University of Freiburg im Breisgau. Coming late in his career, this lecture is a particularly powerful formulation of a position implicitly and at times explicitly maintained by Heidegger since *Being and Time.* Quite simply, it concerns itself with the notion of identity. It begins : "*The usual formulation of the principle of identity reads : A = A.*"[2]. Identity assumes the form of a tautology. In this form, it has been traditionally considered as unworthy of serious inquiry. As is often the case, Heidegger takes the obvious as a challenge. What, he wonders, does it mean that a thing is equal to itself? Plain though the principle may appear, it harbours a series of presuppositions which infiltrate deeply into the foundations of the way we think:

What does the formula A = A state which is customarily used to represent the principle of identity? The formula expresses the equality of A and A. An equation requires at least two elements. One A is equal to another. Is this what the principle of identity is supposed to mean? Obviously not. That which is identical, in Latin "idem", is in Greek τὸ αὐτὸ. Translated, τὸ αὐτὸ means "the same". If someone constantly repeats himself, for example : "the plant is a plant", he speaks in a tautology. For something to be the same, one is always enough. Two are not needed, as they are in the case of equality.[3]

Sameness should not require mediation. Even to say "A = A" seems redundant. And yet, Heidegger argues, the principle of identity has been historically understood as the relation of

---

1. In *Identity and Difference* (New York, Harper and Row, 1969).
2. *Ibid.*, p. 23.
3. *Ibid.*, pp. 23-4.

a thing to itself. Although such a relation is pleonastic, it is necessary. The bizarre conclusion reached by Heidegger is that self-identity is a relation residing precisely where it shouldn't. If anything should be a punctual, instantaneous, and unmediated presence, it should be the identity of an object. In fact, as Derrida has argued, the notion of identity has been historically thought as presence, Heidegger suggests, as does Derrida in the entirety of his work, that identity is not presence, or, stated another way, that presence is not identical to itself:

> The more fitting formulation of the principle of identity "A = A" would accordingly mean not only that every A is itself the same : but rather that every A is itself the same with itself. Sameness implies the relation of "with", that is, a mediation, a connection, a synthesis : the unification into a unity.[4]

Heidegger will proceed to describe two alternative interpretations of the synthesis inherent in identity : speculative Idealism and his own hermeneutic ontology of Being. Although a certain kind of synthesis, specifically a Hegelian *Aufhebung*, would ultimately achieve punctual identity through a process of negation and sublation, for my purposes, I would like to simply focus on Heidegger's provisional conclusion. A thing's identity with itself is a mediation. It is important that this claim be understood for what it is. Heidegger is not saying that a thing may entertain a relation of identity with itself. That is, he is not defining a thing as that which is equal to itself. The metaphor for Heidegger's claim is not Narcissus. We are not to understand identity as an equation signalling the sameness between a thing and itself. Rather, we must take Heidegger's definition literally : "*every A is itself the same with itself.*" A thing's being resides in the mediation offered by the principle of identity. Identity is not the relation between a thing and itself ; identity is that relation which is the condition of possibility of a thing in

4. *Ibid.*, pp. 24-5.

general. That is, identity is constituted through mediation; consequently, mediation is ontologically anterior to identity. Although his conclusion is counter-intuitive, Heidegger's point is clear : in an ontologically primordial way, a relation is not only more basic than what is related, it is also constitutive of what is related. Mediation not only comes first, it also has a generative function. Rather than defining identity as the connection joining a thing and itself, Heidegger argues that it is the relation itself which creates a thing as that which may be encountered.

Although its trajectory is not unencumbered with detours, this reading of *La Chute* passes through four basic phases. Briefly, they are : an enumeration of various images encountered in the first chapter ; a description of the temporality of the two major falls in the novel (the young woman's and Clamence's) ; an analysis of the transformation of the classic confession genre wrought by Clamence, especially as it relates to his revelation of the stolen van Eyck panel ; and a discussion of Clamence's relation to the language he uses.

In order to organize this conclusion, let me summarize the central concerns of each section.

A. *La Chute* is structured by various transmutations of one central system. The seminal metaphor is that of passage. Its very title, *La Chute*, implies a passage from innocence to guilt. The novel is set in Amsterdam. Amsterdam is a port, and, like all ports, it is the site of exchange. That is, a port is a location where goods change hands. Jean-Baptiste Clamence plies his trade in a tawdry bar. He is first encountered as he offers to translate from Dutch to French, or from the inarticulate grunts of the gorilla who presides over the bar into civilized language. As a translator, he is himself the site of exchange. The two kinds of translation he suggests, from one language to another, and from pre-language into civilized discourse, both imply the passage of meaning through a neutral carrier. As a translator, Clamence is supposed to convey an already formed meaning. In fact, the value of a translator is his invisibility. At the limit, a translator would be thoroughly transparent and a message could make its way from one language to another as if there were no detour. In addition to serving as a translator, Clamence is a lapsed lawyer. A lawyer is not necessarily concerned with questions of innocence or guilt. Or rather, his interest is purely teleological. It is at the *end* of a trial that one is declared innocent or guilty. Of course, a trial would be unnecessary if one had access to an omniscient observer. Such a metaphysical eye could decide with certainty all questions of innocence and guilt. Lacking such a searing eye, a court must rely on human deliberation. A lawyer, therefore, must convince a jury (or judge) that his client is innocent. It is only after the lawyer's intervention, and the jury's decision, that the accused is declared innocent or guilty. By manipulating the legal code, and by using language forcibly, a lawyer is potentially able to create the illusion of innocence where there may be none. Clamence does not defend innocent people or criminals ; on the contrary, he seeks to use his rhetorical power to have his clients declared innocent. Innocence and guilt come at the end.

A lawyer is a bridge. He is a bridge between his client and the jury, and between accusation and innocence or guilt. He is a bridge whose right of way is language. Therefore, he is a translator ; whereas a translator would convey meaning, he would convey innocence. Clamence, whether in his role as lawyer or as translator, is what he most fears and what he diligently avoids.

A bridge is both literal and figurative in *La Chute*. Literally, it is the site of numerous harrowing crossings. Whether it is laughter which accosts him, or his own indecision, Clamence is painfully aware of the perils of crossing a bridge. However, insofar as Clamence is himself a bridge, he is himself the site of a hazardous journey. A bridge is both literal and figurative : both, and yet neither, if it is the passage between the two. A bridge is both a metaphor of passage and a metaphor of the metaphor. Coming from the Greek μεταφό-ρειν, to carry over, to transfer, a metaphor has, in the rhetorical sense attributed to it by Aristotle, never ceased to be a conduit. A metaphor transfers sense from one signifier to another. Like Clamence translating from the gorilla's babel into hyper-civilized French, or like a lawyer manipulating a jury as he represents his client, the metaphor is relation in the active sense.

Traditionally, however, the metaphor has been a vehicle for the reappropriation of sense. Being the vacillation between proper and literal meaning, the notion of metaphor is especially vulnerable to Hegelian synthesis[5]. However, understood as language's internal distance, as that primitive space which makes relation thinkable, in short, as that primordial being-outside-itself which inaugurates the possibility of ontology, metaphor is the fissure in all dialectical movements of reintegration[6]. Ultimately, Clamence is a metaphor. He is a metaphor in the pure sense developed by Derrida. That is, he is not a metaphor for any one of a number of traditional categories deployed so deftly by traditional criticism (a metaphor for guilt, for responsibility, for judgment, for Existential angst etc.) but a metaphor for the peculiar notion of linguistic transference encoded in the sign

---

5. Derrida, in « La Mythologie blanche », underlines the metaphor's vulnerablility : « *La métaphore est donc déterminée par la philosophie comme perte provisoire du sens, économie sans dommage irréparable de propriété, détour certes inévitable mais histoire en vue et dans l'horizon de la réappropriation circulaire du sens propre.* » (*Marges*, p. 323).

6. Metaphor, therefore, joins Derrida's battery of deconstructive non-concepts (for example : *gramme, réserve, entame, trace, espacement, supplément, pharmakon, marge, hymen, dissémination, femme, écriture* etc.). Derrida explains : « *L'autre auto-destruction de la métaphore ressemblerait à s'y méprendre à la philosophique* [sic]. *Elle passerait donc cette fois, traversant et doublant la première, par un supplément de résistance syntaxique, par tout ce qui (par exemple, dans la linguistique moderne) déjoue l'opposition du sémantique et du syntaxique et surtout la hiérarchie philosophique qui soumet celui-ci à celui-là. Cette auto-destruction aurait encore la forme d'une généralisation mais cette fois, il ne s'agirait plus d'étendre et de confirmer un philosophème ; plutôt, en le déployant sans limite, de lui arracher ses bordures de propriété. Et par conséquent de faire sauter l'opposition rassurante du métaphorique et du propre dans laquelle l'un et l'autre ne faisaient jamais que se réfléchir et se renvoyer leur rayonnement.* » (p. 323, *Ibid.*).

metaphor.

B. Clamence's fall disrupts the ordinary conceptualization of cause and effect. Normally, if there is a causal relation between two events, they are related temporally as cause preceding effect. In *La Chute*, this unimpugnable sequence is reversed in two ways. Although Clamence's decline begins when he fails to come to the aid of the woman on the pont Royal, the effect of that event remains latent until many years later, when, on another bridge, he hears a mocking laugh behind his back. As if to underline the temporal reversal of Clamence's fall, or perhaps to cause it, *La Chute* presents the two scenes in question reversed from the point of view of absolute temporality but in the correct sequence from the perspective of a certain logic inherent to the novel.

C. Clamence harbours a painting in his cupboard which may or may not be a stolen panel from van Eyck's "The Adoration of the Lamb". Since we are told that it is a perfect copy of the original, and since Clamence has suggested that his relation to truth is more one of inventiveness than of fidelity, the reader and his representative in the novel, the interlocutor, are unable to determine the authenticity of "The Just Judges". This blind spot in a structure of revelation reminiscent of the movement of truth as described by Heidegger is not contingent. That is, it is not cecity which some ray of light may dispatch. No future information, no new fact, can effect a sure identification of the panel. The self-mocking, self-consciously abyssal nature of the text makes such delimitaion of the essence of the painting juridically impossible.

D. The last concern of this analysis is language. Clamence the translator, Clamence the lawyer, and Clamence the confessor are all similar in fetichizing language. However, Clamence warns, a too deft hand with language often masks eczema. This eczema, in turn, is likened to a lack of character. Like the Nazis, who make up for their inner emptiness with method, Clamence uses a finely wrought discourse as a substitute for a deep-seated eczema. Eczema, itself a surface incrustation, is a surface hidden by a surface. Clamence's discourse does not supplant a repulsive content, but an internal surface. As with the Nazis, there are no depths. There is no content to serve as ballast for Clamence's confession. Perhaps Brian T. Fitch sums it up best in « Une Voix qui se parle... ». As I have previously mentioned, his metaphor for Clamence's assault on language is that of the actor for whom the play never ends – the actor with no person behind the thespian's mask:

Les avertissements, à peine voilés, cités plus haut témoignaient déjà du décalage entre le sens apparent des paroles du récit et leur véritable raison d'être, de la distance entre l'acteur et son masque. Cet espace qui sous-tend la trame du récit et qui provient d'un manque d'adhésion psychologique, de sorte que la motivation psychique qu'on serait normalement en droit de déduire de telles paroles fait défaut, est proprement théâtral. [...] il peut être le lieu où résonnent les paroles de l'acteur. C'est ainsi qu'il se manifeste dans les dernières pages du roman.[7]

Lacking psychological depth, Clamence is, according to Fitch, an actor who can never leave the theatre. A confessor who confesses that he lies leaves no landmarks by which to determine the difference between mask and face. His language, although meaningful to a degree, is unable (or unwilling) to point confidently to a stabilizing meaning. Sliding through the ooze of his plastic words, Clamence searches (or seems to search) for a touchstone. But all he can salvage from the energy and parsimoniousness of his discourse is a radically impoverished version of Descarte's Cogito. Instead of establishing the absolute autonomy of the ego, Clamence can, at best, revel in a tautology : I talk therefore I talk. It is the only thing he can be sure of. A judge-penitent is one who has found a recipe, a method like the last recourse of the hollow Nazis.

Having assembled these four areas of concern, my goal is to articulate them. It is for this reason that I inserted

7. Art. cit., pp. 75-6.

Heidegger's *Identity and Difference* into my study. Although Heidegger's book is complex and has concerns ranging far wider than can be ascertained from my selective quotations, it nevertheless makes a powerful statement about the nature of identity. Historically, identity has been understood as preceding difference. That is, difference has always been defined as the difference between beings. Beings, things which are, in general, must exist before they can be compared as either different or the same. Difference is a relation whose presupposition is identity.

Heidegger's reversal of this ontological temporality is radical. Difference, he suggests, is not something befalling already constituted identities ; on the contrary, difference is internal to identity. The notion of identity, Heidegger argues, can only be thought as the consequence of a primordial relation. And, since all relations imply difference, identity is constituted by difference.

As I have explained earlier, this is only the beginning. It is possible to domesticate the violence of internal difference in many ways. For example, Hegel's speculative Idealism seeks to sublate self-exteriorization into a progressively ascending dialectic whose telos is absolute identity. The success or failure of such a project is not my concern. My analysis of *La Chute* is an attempt to demonstrate that a modern novel can, through the creation of an internal, textual, logic, radically question the notion of identity in a way which is analogous to Heidegger's "destruction" of Western Metaphysics.

The four parts of my reading of *La Chute* are themselves components of a larger structure. Fundamentally, the novel is articulated in such a way so as to render inappropriate the use of such concepts as structure, form, content, image etc. Rather than try and establish dichotomies where there are none, I have tried to read the narrative as it presents itself. Not wishing to impoverish the novel through the imposition of critical grids exterior to it, I nevertheless feel that a certain perspective respectful of the text will yield some surprising results.

The fall of the novel's title is from innocence to guilt. Or it is from hypocrisy to lucidity. It matters little. Whether the fall is taken biblically, as the expulsion of Adam and Eve from Eden, or whether it is taken Existentially, as the fall from comfortable bad-faith to the burden of good-faith, the essential topographic structure of the notion of a fall is the same. A fall is the passage from one place or state to another. Consequently, a fall always implies that the origin and destination predate the trajectory connecting them. The minimun requirements for a fall are an origin, a goal, and a vehicle to join them. Furthermore, the origin and destination have traditionally been conceived as autonomous and identical to themselves : the line joining them has been seen as a mere consequence of their presence, much as an electric current will of itself flow from the positive pole of a battery to the negative pole once they are connected with a conductor.

This configuration structures the entirety of Clamence's confession. Whether we consider his role as translator, as lawyer, or as confessor, Clamence is constantly an intermediary. Like the city where he has taken up residence, or like the bar where he accosts potential interlocutors. Clamence is a site of passage and exchange. In that respect, he is not all that different from his menagerie. He too is a fence. When Clamence crosses a bridge, he is crossing a metaphor for himself. And since a bridge is itself a metaphor for the metaphor, then Clamence is a metaphor. The metaphor, therefore, becomes an ecomonic image with which to represent various kinds of passage in *La Chute*.

If Clamence is a bridge, it is because language is his profession. Whatever role he is playing, the potency of his position derives purely from his ability to manipulate language. Language itself is, of course, a bridge. Traditionally, communication has been understood as the transmission of a message from a speaker (or writer) to a listener (or reader)[8]. Furthermore, this transmission has been

8. See R. JAKOBSON, *Essais de linguistique générale* (Paris, Éditions de Minuit, 1963).

conceived as the passage of a pre-formed message from an already constituted sender to an already constituted listener. That is, a message has usually been viewed as an object changing hands, an object having no effect on the hands employed in its transmission.

Communication makes fundamental ontological and temporal assumptions. It assumes that the being of the transmitter is not affected by the message, and that the message is in principle capable of remaining intact during its transmission[9]. In addition, the received concept of communication assumes that a message is conceived by its sender, undergoes a passage, and is finally received and decoded by its recipient. That is, communication presupposes an origin, a passage, and an end. These two components of communication are not unrelated. As Heidegger has demonstrated, ontology, especially in its insistence on the concept of presence, is always temporal. The presence of an object is always understood as deriving its integrity from the punctuality of the present within which it appears. The punctuality of time, especially insofar as it guarantees the discreteness of an origin, is indispensable to any ontology.

What then are the temporal and ontological components of language as it is deployed by Clamence?

Ontologically, language is twice contaminated in *La Chute*. His language, Clamence says, is a mask hiding a void. His well-wrought, slightly precious style is more than language : it is his method, the recipe which he discovered to be capable of circumventing the pain of guilt. Like the Nazi's method, Clamence's use of language both masks a crime and is a

9. Safety of passage and indivisibility are indispensable to the idea of propriety. Referring to Lacan's analysis of "The Purloined Letter", Derrida says : « *Lacan nous reconduit vers la vérité, vers une verité qui, elle, ne se perd pas. Il rapporte la lettre, montre que la lettre se rapporte vers son lieu propre par un trajet propre et, comme il le note expressément, c'est cette destination qui l'intéresse, le destin comme destination.* » (*La Carte postale*, p. 463) and « *Et c'est pourquoi la présupposition intéressée, jamais démontrée, de la matérialité de la lettre comme indivisibilité était indispensable à cette économie restreinte, à cette circulation du propre.* » (*Ibid.*, p. 469).

crime. It is a crime insofar as it communicates no fixed meaning. For Clamence, silence is Greek, language Dutch. His empty style offers no benchmark by which one could judge the truth it purports to convey. At this point in our analysis, we must be especially vigilant in avoiding the meta-phorics of depth, either in their Existentialist (bad-faith/good-faith) or their psychoanalytic (conscious/unconscious) mani-festations. Clamence does not live a schizoid textual existence. The figure of Clamence is not that of a purblind barrister making do. Clamence is not only aware of the slip-pery nature of his language, he admits as much. Part of the vertiginous strategy of judge-penitence is that it is a method which contains, as part of its tactics, the divulgence of its own rules. Clamence's slow and circular narrative is not so much a confession of hypocrisy as an exposition of the artifice of confession. The second problematization of language in *La Chute* occurs when Clamence confesses that confessors confess in order to lie. His admission is neither one of truth or of mendacity. In fact, once he uses this ancient rhetorical ploy, he renders the choice between truth and falsehood inappropriate.

Who, then, is Clamence? I don't mean the question in the naïve, literal sense. As I noted at the beginning, it is a premise of this analysis that the characters of the novel are not to be treated as real people with what is commonly called interiority. But Clamence is a character in a novel, and it is part of the representational schema of the novel genre that characters are lent a certain *textual* reality. Normally, this textual reality is difficult to distinguish from the reality one lends to people in the world. Especially in the realistic novel, the reader is supposed to forget, to a certain degree, that he is reading a novel. Clamence's attitude towards truth makes such a posture impossible. In fact, the narrative strategy of *La Chute* is to refuse to allow itself to be read as anything but text. Ultimately, the interlocutor is not merely the inscrip-tion of the reader within the novel, he is the postulation of the reader as an interpreter of an undecipherable code. As

Brian T. Fitch argues, *La Chute* makes the interlocutor into a reader while it simultaneously deprives him of steady tools with which to go about his work:

But we must not lose sight of the fact that his tale also functions in a completely different fashion with the disappearance of the portrait of a certain Jean-Baptiste Clamence that has turned out to be a complete fabrication : the mirror-portrait has become a mirror and nothing but a mirror. What the reader sees in this mirror is the reflection of his own activity as a reader and an interpreter. Thus it is that the process of autorepresentation is set in motion as it were ; but in such a way that it takes in the hermeneutic activity and operates therefore not on the level of the text-for-itself but on that of the text-for-the-reader. In short, to discover that the interpretation Clamence gives of himself is false is, for the reader, to find himself back where he started from as far as interpreting the character and his story is concerned. The text forces the reader to renew his efforts as an interpreter without providing him with the means to do so. The latter is thrown back upon himself and condemned to going round in circles as he watches himself interpreting while having nothing other than himself to interpret.[10]

Since nothing Clamence says is necessarily so, neither is he. That is, the only access the reader has to Clamence is through language. To the extent that his language is fundamentally abyssal, nothing he says about himself or about his world is to be believed absolutely. But, then again, neither is it to be disbelieved absolutely. Instead of the ancient choice between light and dark, between illumination and ignorance, Clamence's discourse offers the thoroughly modern alternative of a language which makes no truth claims about that which lies outside of itself. *La Chute* is like any other novel. Its distinctiveness is that it is one of the first novels to thematize its own fictionality in a lucid way. Clamence exists in exactly the same way as Goriot. His Amsterdam is as real as Goriot's Paris. People and places in novels (and arguably

10. *The Narcissistic Text*, p. 83.

in the world) are the result of language, not their cause. *La Chute* thematizes the simple yet obstreperous notion that it is the structure of language which creates its speakers and its meanings rather than the inverse. « *Celui-ci* [le sujet] », Reuter argues, « *ne peut plus être constitué de manière extérieure, transcendante au texte. Il est le produit même du discours [...] Clamence est constitué par ce discours.* »[11].

Much as the guilt of a defendant is the result of a thoroughly human, consequently thoroughly limited, decision, so the very notion of identity in *La Chute* is the *result*, not the cause of discourse.

As soon as we begin to use terms such as result and cause, we are squarely in the realm of temporality. *La Chute*'s disruption of the notion of identity has a temporal component. The bridge scenes are described and have their effect in reverse order. But it is not simply a question of inversion. *La Chute* does not gratuitously make effect precede cause. On the contrary, this reversal is essential to the movement of the text. To make effect come first, that is, to make the effect the cause of the cause, is tantamount to demonstrating that language creates the speaker. Specifically, the laughter Clamence hears while crossing the pont des Arts, which is logically the result of his previous refusal to come to the aid of the woman who had leapt off of the pont Royal is, according to the textual logic of Clamence's confession, the cause of what preceded it. Like a criminal, whose guilt *should* have been contemporary with his commission of a crime, but whose guilt is actually determined after the fact, Clamence's guilt is not the result of his failure to jump into the cold waters of the Seine, but of a mocking laughter which first constituted the earlier event as its cause.

The textual temporality of the painting scenes at first appears quite traditional. Although the reader is probably unaware that it is a question of "The Just Judges" the first several times it is suggested, his ignorance is not revolu-

11. *Op. cit.*, p. 48.

tionary. It is actually a modified form of the attitude adopted by the reader of the classic detective story. However, La Chute is fundamentally different from detective fiction. Whereas the detective novel usually ends with the revelation of the identity of the criminal (and his crime), the story of the stolen painting is resolved into a Gordian knot. As opposed to the detective story, there is no Alexander in La Chute to undo the dilemma. The painting is in principle indistinguishable from its copy. Consequently, since there is no sure way to separate original and copy, there is no yardstick with which to measure the distance between production and reproduction. Language also works within the interiority of the punctual self (subject, ego, I etc.). As Husserl has argued, language, even in its most intimate form, interior monologue, is always a presentation ; its status is always secondary to the immediacy of thought which is understood to be simultaneous to the flux of internal temporality[12]. To suggest, following Derrida's lead in L'Origine de la géométrie, that even in the deepest, most cloistered reaches of the transcendental ego, the sanctity of an absolutely punctual origin is infected with a kind of primordial representation, that is, to argue that representation precedes presentation, is to strike the bloodiest possible blow to the ideational system which would confidently separate literature from life.

Clamence's fall is not from one state to another. It is, of course, impossible to dispense with terms such as innocence and guilt, hypocrisy and lucidity, or any one of a series of binary oppositions structuring a typical reading of La Chute. The novel is indeed rife with such dialectics : to ignore them in the name of a transcendental textual reading would be to violate the novel. My reading of La Chute simply suggests an inversion of the ontological assumptions residing in the notion of a fall. Rather than delimiting Clamence's fall as the passage from an origin to a destination, the novel posits this passage as that relation which precedes and is the condition of possibilty for an origin and a telos. We are

12. In Logical Investigations.

not dispensing with these massively metaphysical concepts, so dear to speculative Idealism. I am merely claiming that *La Chute* makes them secondary, derived phenomena. No more than the incident of the pont Royal, origin is not an overflowing source. It is, on the contrary, the product of that which, by all accounts, it should have engendered.

One step remains. Thus far, this reading of *La Chute* has been primarily descriptive. I have sought to read the novel with as much objectivity as that peculiar literary object allows. I have refrained, however, from ascribing a reaction on the part of the novel to the loss of identity it effects. That is, since the novel is a confession, and since a confession creates a character who confesses, it is important to see how the novel also inscribes an attitude towards the violence he perpetrates.

La Chute is peppered with references to the Bible. The metaphorics of innocence and guilt, or, in general, of origin and diaspora, are essentially biblical in nature. Clamence's fall, therefore, is an echo of the central biblical fall, the expulsion of Adam and Eve from Eden. Eden is the origin, it is unmediated presence: « *N'était-ce pas cela, en effet, l'Éden, cher monsieur : la vie en prise directe?* » (1487). Eden is pure punctuality, the total absence of the exteriority of representation. Having discovered that Eden never existed except as the *product* of a certain kind of relation, what is Clamence's reaction?

Two are traditional. Loss is usually accompanied by resentment and/or nostalgia. Although this is not the place to establish a catalogue of reactions to loss, let me simply note that two versions of the combination of resentment and nostalgia are seminal. One is the amalgam of repression, denegation, sublimation, symptom formation etc. constitutive of Freudian psychoanalysis. Whatever the actual mechanics of the model for the psyche being used, whether it is Freudian or Lacanian, for example, the fundamental schema is the same. Loss, actual or imagined, must be made up for. The wounded subject has a battery of substitutes at his disposal, and, depending on the choice, he can be a neurotic, a psychotic, or even relatively normal. Never, however, can he forget the wound gnawing at his centre. Nietzsche presents a deceptively similar model in *Thus Spake Zarathustra*[13]. As he was crossing a bridge, Zarathustra addressed the cripples surrounding him: "*§ A seer, a purposer, a creator, a future itself, and a bridge to the future – and alas! also as it were a dripple on this bridge : all that is Zarathustra*"[14]. Upon a bridge, Zarathustra is himself a bridge. A bridge crossing a bridge, Zarathustra spoke of redemption:

Willing emancepateth : but what is that called which still putteth the emancipator in chains?

"It was" : thus is the Will's teeth-gnashing and lonesomest tribulation called. Impotent towards what hath been done – it is a malicious spectator of all that is past.

Not backward can the Will will ; that it cannot break time and time's desire – that is the Will's lonesomest tribulation.

Willing emancipateth : what doth Willing itself devise in order to get free from its tribulation and mock at its prison?

Ah, a fool becometh every prisoner! Foolishly delivereth itself also the imprisoned Will.

That time doth not run backward – that is its animosity : "That which was" : so is the stone which it cannot roll, called.

And thus doth it roll stones out of animosity and ill-humour, and taketh revenge on whatever doth not, like it, feel rage and ill-humour.

Thus did the Will, the emancipator, become a torturer ; and on all that is capable of suffering it taketh revenge, because it cannot go backward.

This, yea this alone is *revenge* itself : the Will's antipathy to time, and its "It was."[15]

---

13. *The Complete Works of Friedrich Nietzsche*, Oscar Levy ed. (New York, Russel and Russel Inc., 1964).

14. *Ibid.*, p. 167.

15. *Ibid.*, pp. 168-9.

As long as the past is seen as the cause of present misery, the will can only engage in impotent reaction. Zarathustra's solution is to remove the past from the register of the binary opposition origin/derivation. The will, if it is to cleanse itself of revenge, must will the passing of the past :

Away from those fabulous songs did I lead you when I taught you : "The Will is a creator."

All "It was" is a fragment, a riddle, a fearful chance – until the creating Will saith thereto : "But thus would I have it." –

Until the creating Will saith thereto : "But thus do I will it! Thus shall I will it!"

But did it ever speak thus? And when doth this take place? Hath the Will been unharnessed from its own folly?

Hath the Will become its own deliverer and joy-bringer? Hath it unlearned the spirit of revenge and all teeth-gnashing?

And who hath taught it reconciliation with time, and something higher than all reconciliation?

Something higher than all reconciliation must the Will will which is the Will to Power – : but how doth that take place? Who hath taught it also to will backwards?[16]

The creative will, the will to power, is beyond dialectical reconciliation. Its tactic is to will the past, and by willing it, to *retroactively create it*. Creative because it becomes itself the cause of its cause, the will not only breaks the hold of revenge (symptom), but does so lightly. Refusing to deny it, refusing even more to accept it begrudgingly, Zarathustra responds to loss by affirming it[17].

Immediately before he relates the sudden intrusion of the thought of death into his life, Clamence muses about the idea of seriousness. He confesses that he has never been able to take human affairs seriously. Traditionally, truth, or its partner, falsehood, are the only things worthy of seriousness. If one is serious about the loss of truth, then one is still

16. *Ibid.*, p. 170.

17. In *Éperons* (Paris, Flammarion, 1978), Derrida reads Nietzsche's affirmative woman, who is outside the circle of castration and the denial of castration, as a privileged metaphor for « l'écriture ».

operating within the dialectics of truth. The opposite of truth is not falsehood but game. A game is like "life" with one essential difference : whereas the rules of life, its moral, political, linguistic, ideational etc., codes must be perceived as natural if they are to work, the code of a game is posited as artificial and conventional. And, because the regulating principles of a game or sport are fundamentally divorced from that relation to nature which must always accompany and legitimize the metaphysics of truth, Clamence is able to take games seriously:

Je n'ai vraiment été sincère et enthousiaste qu'au temps où je faisais du sport, et, au régiment, quand je jouais dans les pièces que nous représentions pour notre plaisir. Il y avait dans les deux cas une règle du jeu, qui n'était pas sérieuse, et qu'on s'amusait à prendre pour telle. Maintenant encore, les matches du dimanche, dans un stade plein à craquer, et le théâtre, que j'ai aimé avec une passion sans égal, sont les seuls endroits du monde où je me sente innocent.   (1518)

The theatre, where the world is represented in a medium having its own conventions, and sports, a game which arguably imitates life, but which does it in a ritualistic, self-consciously artificial way, are the two events Clamence takes seriously. He inverts the accepted hierarchy ; he treats seriously what is generally posited as frivolous, and conversely, he attacks life with a certain flippancy. Clamence is serious about representation, but unconcerned with what representation represents.

A few pages later, in a previously quoted passage, Clamence distinguishes between his former attitude towards the mortality of truth and a position which is contemporary to the relating of his narrative. If one person alone were to know that what is accepted as true is in fact a lie, then his death would render the lie definitive:

Personne, jamais plus, ne connaîtrait la vérité sur ce point puisque le seul qui la connût était justement le mort, endormi sur son secret. Ce meurtre absolu d'une vérité me donnait le vertige. Aujourd'hui, entre parenthèses, il me donnerait plutôt des plaisirs délicats. L'idée, par exemple, que je suis seul à connaître ce que tout le monde cherche et que j'ai chez moi un objet qui a fait courir en vain trois polices est purement délicieuse. Mais laissons cela. À l'époque, je n'avais pas trouvé la recette et je me tourmentais. (1519)

The set of meanings generated by *La Chute* is structured and organized by the loss of meaning inherent in a journey whose origin and destination are unclear. The truth of the novel, like the truth of "The Just Judges", is contaminated by a primitive unrest. If the scene in which the panel is revealed is a version of the phototropic movement of truth, truth as illumination and truth as correspondence are both reinscribed in *La Chute* as effects parading as causes. But the death of a truth, Clamence claims, no longer revolts him. There is a double irony in Clamence's confession. First, he is of course referring to the painting, consequently he is no longer (nor was he ever) the only person to know what everyone else is ignorant of. Second, Clamence's statement concerning his relation to truth must be read in the context of his claims concerning the truth of his statements. At the very least, Clamence is describing a change in attitude towards the entire problematic of truth. Whereas previously a certain violence against truth was abhorrent to him, as he speaks he finds the prospect of such a violation delicious. His confession, which effects the destabilization of truth he is describing, is a strategy he affirms.

A judge-penitent is one who consciously accepts the limitations of an absolute chasm between consciousness and nature. That loss, whether it be called castration, alienation, or falling, is the loss of something to lose. Loss implies that the thing lost was once possessed. Loss always participates in the same metaphysical structure as possession. It is because loss is a variant of possession, and consequently a reinforcement of the historical notion of possession (material, metaphysical, psychological etc.), that loss is able, through its production of resentment, revenge, repression, displacement etc., to reinstate the ontology of propriety. In its most simple form, the concept of possession requires a metaphysics of *substitutability*. Possession must be either eternal or capable of returning eternally, even if its return is in symptoms, fetishes, or metaphors in general[18]. *La Chute* suggests an alternative. It suggests that the greatest loss of all, the loss which is the model for loss in general, can be affirmed. It suggests that the loss of nature as confirmation, prototype, and source, can be removed from the psychoanalytic category of trauma ; it suggests that from the perspective of a bridge, convention in general (language, strategy, recipe, code etc.) may be affirmed as the source of that striking oxymoron, the concept of nature.

If nature is a concept, if nature is an effect rather than a cause, then any attempt to accede to it is doomed to belatedness : « *Il est trop tard, maintenant, il sera toujours trop tard.* » (1549). In the face of a structural and unablatable delay, Clamence is left to weave an endlessly proliferating text as a monument to his efforts to leave it. Ultimately, however, there is only the book. And Clamence, who has always known that his is narrating himself, is pleased that it is too late to finish his story.

If *La Chute* can be said to end, I choose to take the narrator's last word, « *Heureusement!* » (1549), as something less than sarcasm.

18. In *What Is Called Thinking* (New York, Harper and Row, 1972), Heidegger criticizes Nietzsche's eternal return of the same (the will to power's willing its own "It was" eternally) as a metaphysical fragment.

BIBLIOGRAPHY OF WORKS CITED

1. Books on Camus

BOUSQUET, François, *Camus le méditerranéan Camus l'ancien* (Sherbrooke, Québec, Éditions Naaman, 1977).

BRISVILLE, Jean-Claude, *Camus* (Paris, Gallimard, coll. « Bibliothèque Idéale », 1959).

COSTES, Alain, *Albert Camus ou la parole manquante : Étude psychologique* (Paris, Payot, coll. « Science de l'Homme », 1973).

FITCH, Brian T., *The Narcissistic Text. A Reading of Camus' Fiction* (Toronto, University of Toronto Press, coll. "Romance Series", 1982).

GADOUREK, Carina, *Les Innocents et les coupables : essai d'exégèse de l'œuvre d'Albert Camus* (The Hague, Mouton, 1963).

GASSIN, Jean, *L'Univers symbolique d'Albert Camus : Essai d'interprétation psychanalytique* (Paris, Lettres Modernes, coll. « La Thèsothèque », 1980).

MAILHOT, Laurent, *Albert Camus ou l'imagination du désert* (Montréal, Les Presses de l'Université de Montréal, 1973).

MASTERS, Brian, *Camus : a Study* (Totowa, New Jersey, Rowman and Littlefield, 1974).

REUTER, Yves, *Texte/idéologie dans* La Chute *de Camus* (Lettres Modernes, coll. « Archives des Lettres Modernes », 1980).

REY, Pierre-Louis, *Camus:* La Chute (Paris, Hatier, coll. « Profil d'une œuvre », 1970).

Albert Camus, n° 3, « Sur *La Chute* », 1970.

2. Other Books

The American Heritage Dictionary of the English Language (Boston, Houghton Mifflin, 1979).

BELLEMIN-NOËL, Jean, Psychanalyse et littérature (Paris, PUF, 1978).

BELLEMIN-NOËL, Jean, Vers l'inconscient du texte : « Écriture » (Paris, PUF, 1978).

De MAN, Paul, Blindness and Insight (New York, Oxford University Press, 1971).

DERRIDA, Jacques, La Carte postale (Paris, Flammarion, 1980).

DERRIDA, Jacques, L'Écriture et la différence (Paris, Seuil, 1967).

DERRIDA, Jacques, Éperons (Paris, Flammarion, 1978).

DERRIDA, Jacques, Marges de la philosophie (Paris, Éditions de Minuit, 1973).

DERRIDA, Jacques, L'Origine de la géométrie (Paris, PUF, 1962).

DERRIDA, Jacques, La Voix et le phénomène (Paris, PUF, 1972).

FREUD, Sigmund, Complete Psychological Works, ed. James Strachey (London, Hogarth Press, 1954).

FREUD, Sigmund, The Origins of Psychoanalysis (New York, Basic Books, 1964).

HEIDEGGER, Martin, Being and Time (New York, Harper and Row, 1962).

HEIDEGGER, Martin, Identity and Difference (New York, Harper and Row, 1969).

HEIDEGGER, Martin, Poetry, Language and Thought (New York, Harper and Rowe, 1971).

HEIDEGGER, Martin, What is Called Thinking (New York, Harper and Row, 1972).

HUSSERL, Edmund, Idées directices pour une phénoménologie (Paris, Gallimard, 1950).

HUSSERL, Edmund, Logical Investigations (New York, Humanities Press, 1970).

JAKOBSON, Roman, Essai de linguistique générale (Paris, Éditions de Minuit, 1963).

LACAN, Jacques, Écrits (Paris, Seuil, 1966).

NIETZSCHE, Friedrich, The Complete Works, ed. Oscar Levy (New York, Russel and Russel, 1964).

SAUSSURE, Ferdinand de, Cours de linguistique générale (Paris, Payot, 1965 [1915]).

3. Articles

BLANCHOT, Maurice, « La Confession dédaigneuse », *N.N.R.F.*, n° 48, déc. 1956, pp. 1050-6.

FITCH, Brian T., « Une Voix qui se parle, qui nous parle, que nous parlons, ou l'espace théâtral de *La Chute* », *Albert Camus*, n° 3, « Sur *La Chute* », 1970, pp. 59-79.

GASSIN, Jean, « *La Chute* et le retable de 'L'Agneau mystique' : Étude de structure » in *Albert Camus 80*, ed. Raymond Gay-Crosier (Gainesville, University Presses of Florida, 1980), pp. 133-9.

LAKICH, John J., "Tragedy and Satanism in Camus' *La Chute*", *Symposium*, vol. XXIV, no. 3, "Albert Camus II", Fall 1970, pp. 262-76.

MEYERS, Jeffrey, "Camus' *The Fall* and van Eyck's 'The Adoration of the Lamb'", *Mosaic*, vol. VII, no. 3, 1974, pp. 43-51.

QUILLIOT, Roger, « *Albert Camus ou les difficultés du langage* », *Albert Camus*, n° 2, « Langue et langage », 1969, pp. 77-102.

QUILLIOT, Roger, « Clamence et son masque », *Albert Camus*, n° 3, « Sur *La Chute* », 1970, pp. 81-100.

WHARTENBY, H. Allen, "The Interlocutor in *La Chute*", *PMLA*, vol. LXXXIII, no. 5, Oct. 1968, pp. 1326-33.

Littérature, « Le Roman policier », févr. 1983.